THE MESSAGE OF
Jonah

THE MESSAGE OF

Jonah

A Theological
Commentary

TERENCE E. FRETHEIM

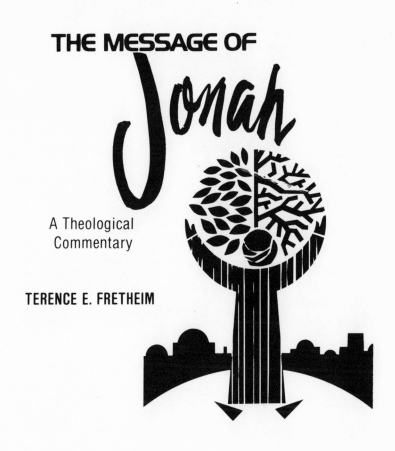

AUGSBURG PUBLISHING HOUSE
MINNEAPOLIS, MINNESOTA

CONTENTS

To
my mother and father
who first taught me the Scriptures

PREFACE

There is a general lack of literature on Old Testament books that tries to move between the more technical, scholarly work and a devotional type of literature (both of which are much needed). This book attempts to fill that gap, in a manner similar to a previous book, *Creation, Fall and Flood: Studies in Genesis 1-11* (Augsburg, 1969). It concentrates on what I believe to be the most important aspects of Jonah, its theological and kerygmatic content. This means leaving somewhat to the side, though not forgetting, the detailed work with the text so necessary to capture its theology and message well.

Lectures first delivered to pastors' conferences in Minnesota and Montana provide the nucleus for this book. Classes at Luther Seminary provided another proving ground for this material. I am indebted to all those involved for their questions, comments and suggestions. It is a better book because of that interchange.

Because of the nature of the book it is impossible to give adequate credit to all the books and articles which have taught me much about Jonah. A few of the most important will be mentioned along the way (and listed in the brief bibliography at the end of the book).

I would like, however, to cite several special sources here. My most basic perspective on Jonah has been shaped by a book of sermonic materials by Richard Luecke (*Violent Sleep,* 1969). My more technical understandings of Jonah have been most informed by the work of a German scholar, H. W. Wolff (*Studien zum Jonabuch,* 1965). Some conversations with Professor Wolff in Heidelberg, Germany, brought home those insights to me.

I would also like to call special attention to two commentaries on Jonah, that of L. C. Allen in the *New International Commentary* Series (Eerdmans) and that of H. W. Wolff, a manuscript of which was kindly loaned to me by Professor Wolff. Though they were received after my work was virtually completed, both were very helpful in the final polishing process and are to be highly recommended for further study.

The basic groundwork for some of my own perspectives on Jonah may be located in an article in *Zeitschrift für die alttestamentliche Wissenschaft* (1978), "Jonah and Theodicy."

I would like to thank Luther Theological Seminary and its Board of Regents for granting me a sabbatical leave during which time this work could be completed. Gratitude is also due to Aid Association for Lutherans of Appleton, Wisconsin, for providing me with a generous sabbatical grant. I would also like to thank Dr. Daniel Simundson for his positive evaluation of the manuscript.

Finally, special thanks must go to my wife, Faith, whose constant support has been a source of great encouragement to me.

I

FINDING

THE

FOCUS

More often than not the big fish has gotten all the attention. This is as true today as in any past generation. Ask Christians or Jews, or any person on the street for that matter, what the book of Jonah is all about. The fish will figure prominently in most replies.

This has often had some unfortunate results. For those without religious ties this has meant that the book could be easily dismissed as ridiculous and undeserving of serious attention. The "story of the big fish" has thus for generations served as a convenient (though quite improper) "stumbling block" over against the Judeo-Christian faith. For the serious Bible student, on the other hand, the book has often been used as a touchstone of orthodoxy. Quite apart from the question of the meaning of the book, recognition of the sheer "happenedness" of the miracle of the fish has been made a necessity for the person who would be a true believer.

Both of these perspectives, however, tend to ignore the fact that the miracle of the fish plays a relatively minor role in the story (it is mentioned in only three verses!). Moreover, commonly betraying minimal acquaintance with the book as a whole, they have been prone to shift attention away from the more significant aspects of the book and the question of its message then and now.

A kind of historicism has often been allowed to prevail, where the message of the book has been significantly diminished or lost altogether in the search for what did (or did not!) happen. It seems to be commonly thought that once the historicity of the book has been established (or denied) that everything important about the book has thereby been stated. But it cannot be stressed strongly enough that, whatever one's decision on the matter of historicity, the question of the message of the book has at that point hardly begun to be discerned.[1]

Retelling the Story

To assist in the process of finding the proper focus of the book, it may be helpful to begin with a retelling of the story. There is, of course, no substitute for reading the original! Yet putting the story into a more modern idiom may help us understand the book. It could also lead to misunderstanding, but that is the risk any modern interpreter or translator takes.

There he was. Jonah was just there. Probably doing what he had always been in the habit of doing. When out of the blue, like a sudden, sharp pain in the stomach, a strange word is heard. "Take a trip to Nineveh and tell them their time is up. They have gone too far. Their sins have found them out."

In obvious agitation Jonah packs his bags and sets off for . . . the harbor! He spots a ship going away from Nineveh and buys the most expensive ticket they've got. "I cannot take up such a task. Moreover, I will remove myself to a spot on this earth where I will no longer have to listen to such possibilities. Maybe after a few years . . ."

God does not take such a response indifferently. He whips up a mighty wind on the sea. A storm rages. The boat is tossed about like a cork in a tidal wave. It is on the verge of breaking up. The pagan sailors are in a tizzy, shouting prayers to the sky as they throw the cargo overboard. Perhaps the gods will be appeased. The noise and tumult of sea and sailors pounds upon the ear. And Jonah sleeps like a baby.

Jonah is startled awake by the captain himself. "Hey! Why aren't you praying like the rest of us? Maybe *your* god will consider our plight and save us." Jonah responds with silence.

The situation deteriorates. Measures other than those used thus far must be taken. "There must be someone on board who has offended his god. Let's throw the dice and find out who it is." Jonah's number comes up. With the wind heaping up the waves, Jonah is stormed with questions. Backed into a corner, he finally speaks. He makes his origins and religious loyalties known. My God is the Lord and I am fleeing from him.

The sailors react more fearfully to Jonah's confession than they had to the storm initially. How could Jonah speak and behave as he does! They are really in trouble! The sailors press him for a solution. The storm is getting worse. How does one go about pacifying such a god?!

Jonah now knows that there is no simple way out. He admits that he is the cause of the storm and has gotten the sailors into this jam. Yet he refuses to repent. And so he devises a plan that, while justly saving the sailors, challenges God to act in a similarly just way: Throw me overboard!

Nevertheless, the sailors show concern for Jonah by attempting to find another solution. But they are unsuccessful in their attempt to row to land. Realizing that they have no other way out, they pray to Jonah's God, gently reminding him that this is his solution and not theirs. They do not want to be held responsible. They throw Jonah overboard and the storm stops. The sailors then place their trust in Jonah's God and worship him in ways appropriate for any Jew.

Meanwhile, Jonah is on his way to the bottom. The darkness of the deep engulfs him. He becomes all entangled in the seaweed. In the depths of the sea death seems inevitable. But Jonah cries out to God for help. God hears his prayer and sends a savior. A fish saves Jonah from drowning and transports him back toward home. On the way Jonah sings a song of thanksgiving to God for his deliverance. He vows to worship him in all the appropriate ways upon his return home. After a three-day journey the fish vomits Jonah up—head over heels upon the sand dunes. He is now back where he can once again be called to take up his task.

And once again the call does come. It is the same as the first one. This time Jonah goes, though he keeps his reasons to himself. He arrives at the large city of Nineveh and walks only part way into it, crying his simple little message of doom as he goes: "In forty days Nineveh will become like Sodom and Gomorrah!"

The response is overwhelming. Everybody in town, from nobleman to peasant, believes in God. The news reaches the king and he, too, responds in faith. He removes his royal clothes, sits in penitence before the king of kings, and puts the royal stamp of approval upon the spontaneous reaction of the people. He issues a decree making it "government policy." Even the animals of the city are to participate in the fasting and offering of prayers to God. All are to turn away from their evil ways. Faith in God and violence don't mix.

The king remains uncertain as to what is going to happen. He knows that God is not somehow obligated to turn away from his wrath. Yet he is hopeful that God will respond in gracious fashion.

And God does just that. When God sees how they have responded, God freely changes his mind with regard to the threatened destruction. In his mercy he lets Nineveh live.

But Jonah becomes very angry at this turn of events. If God will not be angry at the wicked Ninevites when he should be, then Jonah will. And Jonah lets God know exactly how he feels. This result was, of course, what Jonah was afraid of from the very beginning. That was why he tried to escape from the call to go to Nineveh. He knew, he just knew, that God had a soft spot in his heart. If the wicked Ninevites showed any positive response to his preaching, God would not let them get what they deserved—a just reward for their evil deeds. If God is not going to relate himself to people in ways that are consistent with their conduct, then God is capricious and life is absurd. In such a situation death is much to be preferred.

But God, rather than taking Jonah's life, mercifully comes to him. He asks Jonah whether his anger is a proper response, whether he is right in passing judgment on God's decision not to be angry. Jonah treats the question with utter silence. He builds himself a hut outside of the city, and obstinately sets himself in his point of view, challenging God to do with the city what in justice ought to be done.

God responds this time with action rather than speech. His purpose is to move Jonah away from his obstinate perspective. A plant is provided for Jonah to shelter him from the sun. Jonah reacts with great joy at these developments. But then God almost immediately sends a worm to kill the plant and a hot east wind to make life miserable for Jonah.

Again Jonah expresses the desire to die. God was visiting him with destruction while he let the Ninevites live. Once again God comes with a question. Was it right for him to be angry because the plant had been destroyed? Was it right for him to pass judgment on God's act of taking away the plant? After all, it wasn't really *his* plant at all. He had not somehow earned it in the first place. He had not created it or nurtured it. Moreover, his ties to it were obviously superficial—it had grown up and perished in a single day. The plant was a gift, pure and simple.

If the plant was an undeserved gift, and Jonah had no claims upon it at all, then he had no right to be angry at God or to call God's actions into question. But inasmuch as Jonah had chosen to respond in this way in any case, then surely he should recognize *God's* right to respond as he willed with his creatures, the Ninevites.

God in his mercy chose to have pity on the Ninevites rather

than allow destruction to overwhelm them. As sovereign Creator, this was his free right to do, without having Jonah or any other creature call that right into question. Moreover, such divine action meant that God took Nineveh's deserved suffering upon himself. Should Jonah begrudge such generosity?

A Central Figure?

We now need to proceed further with our question regarding the focus of the book. If it is not the fish, it could be Jonah. As we shall see in the next chapter, Jonah is indeed the most important figure in the book. Yet, whatever one's view on the historicity of the book (see below, Chapter V), the author is not interested in writing a biography of Jonah. Nor is he simply desirous of giving us a study of his own generation by mirroring them in the figure of Jonah.

Moreover, the author is not concerned about problems with prophets in general, of whom Jonah is a representative. It has been suggested that Jonah was concerned that his prediction regarding the destruction of Nineveh would not come true.[2] Thus he would be made to look like a false prophet in the eyes of his contemporaries. When this does in fact occur, however, a discussion between Jonah and God follows in Chapter 4 without any reference to prophecy. Moreover, neither the word prophet nor any related word occurs in the book (see below, Chapter II). The center of attention is quite removed from prophecy as such. Also it was generally recognized in Israel that a word spoken by a prophet was contingent (see Jeremiah 18:7-11), that is, it would come to pass only in the light of the way the people responded to the message.

Is God, then, the central figure? There is certainly a sense in which this is true. It is God's actions which make for much of the movement in the book. He calls Jonah to go to Nineveh in both Chapter 1 and Chapter 3, on the basis of which everything happens. He hurls the storm, which sets the next two chapters into motion. Clear statements about his creative and redemptive works are given in the book (1:9, 4:2), and the whole seems permeated with the notion of God's sovereignty and readiness to have mercy.

Yet this, too, is one-sided. This is so, because the first three verses of the book make it clear that what is at the center of the book's attention is a problem *between* God and Jonah.

A Theological Conflict

The first verses of the book set the stage for what follows (see below, Chapter IV). God calls Jonah to go and preach to the Ninevites and Jonah refuses. It is of crucial importance to recognize that what is at issue here is *not* that Jonah is a former man of faith whom God seeks to convert. God's call comes to a man of faith and Jonah does not cease to be such the moment he decides to refuse the call. He is disobedient, but such an action does not immediately remove him from the relationship with God (there wouldn't be any people of God if that were the case!). Jonah is a member of the Israelite community of faith. His God is the Lord.

Jonah then runs away from God not because of unbelief or an absence of faith. Rather he decides to flee because of a certain *belief* which he has.[3] In other words, Jonah is a "runaway believer." The issue in the book then is one between a man of faith and his God. It is an issue which involves an *interpretation* of an aspect of the meaning of that relationship. It is a *theological conflict*.

It is this theological conflict which leads him first of all into disobedience and then finally into despair. This is a witness to what effect wrong beliefs can have on all aspects of life (see below, Chapters VI, IX). This makes it clear that Jonah's disobedience and despair are only *symptoms* of a more basic problem stemming from a theological position which is wrong, but which he holds dearly.

To recognize this has important implications for the interpretation of the book. This means, for example, that God's actions in the book are not directed toward re-integrating Jonah into the community of believers. He is not even *fundamentally* concerned with getting Jonah to be obedient to his commands. For even after Jonah is obedient (3:3) the issue remains. This was a matter secondary to the larger issue, and would be placed in proper perspective once the theological problem was settled.

But this means, of course, that the *obedience* of Jonah in certain situations would not necessarily indicate that the theological conflict had been resolved. Thus, for example, even though it is stated in 3:3 that Jonah went to Nineveh "according to the Word of the Lord," that is no sign that the issue has been cleared up. His disobedience was only a symptom in the first place. It, of course, becomes immediately clear in Chapter 4 that this is the case.

To recognize this also means that Jonah's words and actions will take on a particular hue. He is a divided man. He will give signs of being a man of faith as well as signs of one who is in theological conflict (with its accompanying symptoms). Thus one should not be at all surprised to see Jonah praying (see 2:1, 4:2), though the conflict will no doubt affect the character of Jonah's life of prayer. And we should also not be surprised if he should confess the faith of the Israelite community (see 1:9, 4:2), because not everything that is a matter of belief in his life would have been suddenly suspended. While that confession of faith would no doubt be affected by the conflict, this implies that the psalm should not be discounted as being inappropriate in the mouth of Jonah (see below, Chapters IV, VII).

This explains much regarding the methods which God uses with Jonah. God's actions throughout are directed first and foremost toward the resolution of the theological conflict.

Thus God does not preach to Jonah, seeking to reveal to him what he has done. Jonah *knows* what he is doing. He runs with his eyes wide open. Diagnosis is not in order. Moreover, God does not warn Jonah where his actions will lead him. Jonah *knows* what the consequences of his actions could be. Yet he sleeps like a baby. Threats or simple words of judgment are thus not in order.

Rather, God acts silently to begin with, though not passively. He sends wind and storm. He maneuvers the lots of the heathen. He commands a fish to do his will. By such actions he reveals his sovereignty over all of creation. God is involved throughout the wide world in the carrying out of his purposes, not just in Israel or in places chosen by Israel. No restrictive or partial human perspectives can presume to limit his activity or finally frustrate his saving purposes. This activity thus lays the groundwork for the subsequent discussion (in Chapter 4).

Particularly important among these actions of God are those judgmental and redemptive acts which Jonah himself experiences. God lets Jonah experience his judgment (on and in the sea) so that he might know at first hand what judgment is like. And then he delivers Jonah from the sea quite apart from the question of whether the disobedient Jonah *deserves* to be delivered. Jonah thus becomes the recipient of God's grace in a way no different from what would be the case for Nineveh. God's involvement in the life of Jonah thus becomes the paradigm or model over against which God's activity among the Ninevites (or anyone else) should be judged. If Jonah, why not Nineveh? If Israel, why not Nineveh?

God thus acts without a word until he has brought Jonah to the point where he can *discuss* the matter with him. Because the issue between God and Jonah is a theological one, it finally requires *theological discussion* to move toward resolution. This discussion is accompanied by divine actions which essentially recapitulate God's previous actions of judgment and deliverance (he sends the plant and then destroys it). God's ways with Jonah fit his case admirably. The book thus reveals a God who adjusts the patterns of his actions in deed and word according to the needs of his people.

We now need to ask into the theological issue that makes for this conflict between god and Jonah.

The Theological Issue

It is often thought that the conflict between God and Jonah centers primarily around the question of Israel's mission to the Gentiles.[4] Thus, the chosen people (Jonah) have become exclusivistic regarding their faith, neglecting their responsibilities in mediating the blessing they had received to others. As such, the book would be understood as a forceful reminder of this task of mission.

This task is almost certainly within the purview of the author, but it emerges indirectly and needs to be carefully stated. Nowhere in the book is a radical Gentile/Jew dichotomy stated or implied. Jonah's stated reasons for not obeying God's command (4:2) are not at all related to the non-Jewishness of the Ninevites. It is always their violence or wickedness which is in view (1:2, 3:9, 10). Moreover, Jonah's attitude toward the heathen sailors in Chapter 1 is quite positive. In fact, his response to them in 1:12 (see below, Chapter VI), making their deliverance possible as a matter of justice, clearly eliminates the possibility of ascribing a radically exclusivistic perspective to Jonah.

Yet it also needs to be stated that something would be lost if a city populated with wicked and violent *Jews* were to be substituted for Nineveh. Moreover, to replace the pagan sailors with Jews would significantly change the character of the book. In some way the message of the book concerns the relationship between Israel and non-Jewish people who could be represented both by the pagan sailors and by the wicked Ninevites. Moreover, the indispensable role that Jonah plays in the change of the pagan sailors in Chapter 1 relates in some way to the problems and possibilities of Israel's relationship to other peoples. Yet, this concern must be placed in a context shaped primarily by considerations detailed below.

It has also been suggested that the word addressed to Israel relates to the incomprehensibility of God's actions in the world.[5] For Jonah, God cannot be depended upon absolutely. He repents, he changes his mind (see below, Chapter VIII). An element of uncertainty is thus introduced into God's ways with his creatures, making life miserable for them. The book was thus intended to make clear that God's actions are finally impenetrable to human insight, a situation with which the community of faith must learn to live.

But the issue for Jonah is not so much *that* God repents, but *for whom* he repents.[6] Jonah is certainly aware that Israel's very life depended upon God's willingness to change his mind, to be merciful rather than simply just. Jonah had no problem with God's changeableness per se. Jonah's problem is the *indiscriminate* extension of God's repentance to other people. As has been noted above, his resistance is not related to sharing God's deliverance with the heathen as such. It is only his sharing his mercy with *certain* heathen, namely, those whose cup of evil had been filled to overflowing, "whose wickedness has come up before God" (1:2; cf. Joel 3:13; Isaiah 10:5-19).

Jonah's complaint concerns the leniency granted to the guilty. Nineveh had taken up the sword (more than any other known!) and should, if *anyone* should, perish by the sword. Jonah, who had announced the greatness of Israel's future (2 Kings 14:25), was now being called upon to offer a future to the very country that had put an end to that glorious vision of Jonah's (see 2 Kings 17).

To Jonah this must have been sheer madness. Such a circumvention of all that goes by the name of justice! In the face of such injustice what difference does faith make after all (see below, Chapter II)? For Jonah, God, if he is to be truly God and if Israel's faith is to be meaningful, must conform to canons of righteousness that relate divine response to human conduct in ways that are consistent, if not predictable. The good life should be rewarded, and the bad life should be made to reap its proper fruit. That's only fair!

Thus the theme of God's changing his mind must remain tied to that of God's slowness to anger in the face of horrendous evil (as in 4:2). For Jonah, when the time for judgment has come, it should not be delayed (see Jeremiah 25:15ff.). As it was with the northern kingdom in 721 B.C. (see 2 Kings 17:17) and with Judah in 587 B.C. (see 2 Kings 24:3-4, "And the Lord did *not* pardon"), so should it also be with Nineveh (see Jeremiah 30:23-24). Any other course of action on God's part would be unjust.

The basic theological issue between God and Jonah then is the question of God's justice, God's not treating people according to what they deserve. God is much too free with his mercy in his dealings with people. God should be more strict in his application of the rules of the moral order of life which he himself has ordained in the first place.

Thus, for Jonah, when it comes to the question of mission, it is a matter of *limiting* the breadth and depth of the task. God's message should be extended only to a restricted audience. Truly wicked people such as the Ninevites should be excluded from the possibility of responding positively to the Word of God. They should simply be allowed to suffer the consequences of their own behavior without a chance for deliverance.

The author disagrees with Jonah, of course, and seeks to show why Jonah is wrong in this conflict he is having with God. Basically it can be said that he seeks to dissolve Jonah's arguments (see below, Chapter IX). Everything Israel has is a gift from God, given to her quite apart from the question of justice. Israel herself (and Jonah, in Chapters 2 and 4:6) has not deserved God's acts of deliverance. God's actions toward her have always gone beyond the question of justice, beyond the careful calculation of what she has deserved. Hence the loss of what has been given to Israel, or giving what Israel has to others, should not become an occasion for accusing God of being unfair in his dealings with people.

An appeal is thus made to God's sovereignty. Jonah is creature, not Creator. As such he has no right to make ultimate judgments regarding his fellow creatures. God as Creator is sovereign and he has the right to do what he pleases regarding Nineveh, or anyone else. But in all that he does he will be primarily concerned about extending love and mercy to his creatures, so that his saving purposes might be accomplished.

God's word of judgment is not thereby reduced to a phantom, however, to a bare threat with no teeth in it. Sinful behavior will indeed lead to death rather than life. But this is not what God wants for *any* of his creatures. And thus his actions (and the actions he desires on the part of his people) are always informed by his desire to bring the gift of life and salvation to all.

It is within this larger context, then, that the "missionary message" of the book must be placed. No one is to be excluded from the salvation purposes of God for his creation (see Romans 3:29). Israel has no claim on God's salvation that would enable her to set anyone else outside, even the most wicked among the peoples of the world (see Isaiah 56:6-8; 19:19-25). God is eager to respond to one and all (see Isaiah 65:1). All are his creatures and his saving purposes encompass each one.

At the same time his saving purposes cannot be fully realized apart from Israel's cooperation. God will not *inevitably* pity Nineveh. Nineveh is not spared irrespective of her response (see 3:10), and her response is made possible only by Israel's mediation (as also in the case of the sailors).

This, however, is a missionary message in a broad rather than a narrow sense. It is nowhere stated that the heathen sailors or the Ninevites are (to be) incorporated into the covenant community of Israel.[7] In contrast to most other related Old Testament passages (see, e.g., Isaiah 2:2-4; 60:1-14), the heathen do not come to Jerusalem.

A centripetal understanding of mission here gives way to a centrifugal perception (cf. Genesis 28:14). Israel is to place herself at the service of other peoples in extending the message of

God's Word. But such *extension* does not entail her own *expansion*. Jonah's contemporaries would have to learn that while Israel is the people of God, the people of God is broader than Israel. While Israel remains the focal point for the extension of God's Word to all, in such suffering service she loses any exclusive claim to be the people of God.

Thus, in the process of resolving a conflict, the author addresses a two-pronged Word of God to his contemporaries.

It is first and foremost a word regarding the mercy of God. God's mercy is available to all and is not subject in its application to careful calculation according to human customs and preferences. Israel, too (perhaps above all!), needs to hear anew that God's merciful actions toward her constitute a gift. She lives by grace alone!

But the author's message also carries a word of responsibility. All of the positive responses of the heathen in Chapters 1 and 3 show what reactions are possible if only Israel will open her life to the world. The world of God's creation is given to Israel as a field of vision. It becomes their world because it is his. All of its creatures are to be opened up to the kind of life Israel has received because they are creatures of God and are included within his salvific purposes. Because they are the objects of his love and concern, they are to be the objects of Israel's love and concern, no matter how violent or evil they may be.

The Book of Jonah is thus the Word of God calling forth a response from his people, challenging them to a new understanding of the breadth of his mercy and providential care, as well as a new perception of what this means as regards their responsibilities in the world.

Notes

1. We perhaps need to be reminded that such historicism is just as much evident in those who concern themselves largely with denying the historical character of the book as with those whose main concern is establishing its historicity.

2. See E. Feuillet, "Le Sens du livre de Jonas," *Revue Biblique,* 54 (1947), pp. 343-46. This point of view is already rejected by Luther, *Luther's Works,* vol. 19, pp. 49-50.

3. See R. Luecke, *Violent Sleep,* pp. 6-8.

4. See G. Knight, *Ruth and Jonah,* rev. ed., SCM, 1966.

5. See A. Jepsen, "Anmerkungen zum Buche Jona," in *Wort-Gebot-Glaube,* Festschrift W. Eichrodt, 1971, p. 300.

6. See my article, "Jonah and Theodicy," in *Zeitschrift für die alttestamentliche Wissenschaft,* 90 (1978), pp. 227-237.

7. Cf. L. C. Allen, *The Books of Joel, Obadiah, Jonah and Micah,* pp. 190, 194: "If the book is no missionary tract, it is an important contribution to the prolegomena of a theology of mission."

II

JONAH
AS SUBJECT
AND OBJECT

It is rightly suggested that Jonah is a figure used by the author as a vehicle for describing his own contemporaries. That is, Jonah's thoughts and actions are sketched by the author in such a way as to parallel those of the audience to which the book is addressed.[1] In so doing, he writes to bring about change in the hearts and minds of his readers. Thus it may be said that the author's audience is not only the object of the book's message, but also, insofar as their lives are parallel to Jonah's, the subject of the book. The book is written not only for them but about them.

Our basic task in this chapter is to describe the figure of Jonah as he appears in the book. This will enable us to get some picture of the primary audience to which the book is directed. On this basis some attempt may then be made to determine the historical setting for the book. But, first of all, it is necessary to justify our conclusion that Jonah is a type of the author's audience. We will again be pushed in this direction by the typological significance we see attached to the name Nineveh.

Jonah, the Typical Israelite

We will see (in Chapter III below) that Jonah is a name which the author borrows from 2 Kings 14:25 because it provides a helpful starting point for dealing with the question of the justice of God raised by his contemporaries. Israel had been destroyed by Nineveh (see 2 Kings 17) and now an Israelite prophet was called upon to offer life to the destroyer. (This, of course, presumes a date for the book after the fall of Israel in 721 B.C. To this we will turn below.) How unfair that must have seemed, not only to Jonah but to any Israelite. This is to say that Jonah's reaction to the commission given him by God could not help but have been that of any good Israelite. It was such an extreme case. Thus, the typical Israelite would have immediately identified himself with Jonah.

The author assists in this identification process in a number of ways. He gives just enough information about Jonah (the name of the father) for the audience to be able to catch the connections in 2 Kings. He then leaves unspoken all other possible ties between Jonah and that historical period throughout the rest of the book. This, of course, greatly assists in the process of identification. The most surprising omission of all perhaps is that Jonah is nowhere identified as a prophet. Such an omission would enable a more thoroughgoing identification with Jonah on the part of those who were not prophets. Yet, at the same time, the connection with the historical prophet in just the opening verse would have enabled the audience to conclude immediately that they were not dealing with some oddball or unbeliever. Jonah being a prophet of God was clearly a man of faith.

Moreover, every statement directed to Jonah in the book is a question or includes a question. This literary technique serves to draw the reader into identity with Jonah still further. In the final chapter the identity factor is sharpened by God himself becoming Jonah's questioner. This questioning process is then brought to a climax in the last verses of the book, where the readers are left with a question that necessitates a response to the central conflict of the book. Thus the questions provide an excellent means by which the listener can be drawn progressively more deeply into the story and see it finally as a story about himself.

The Figure of Jonah

If then the picture of Jonah sketched by the author is descriptive of those to whom the book is addressed, we must now make such a characterization. This will enable us to see the shape of that audience. And the more we know about the audience, the better we will be able to see the message of the book, the message those people needed to hear. And perhaps a message that we need to hear.

Some descriptions of Jonah have been almost exclusively negative. They have centered on his flight, his disobedience of the call to be God's messenger, his anger at the conversion of Nineveh, and his obstinacy in the face of God's questioning. These elements should not be discounted, but such a characterization is much too one-sided. There are positive aspects to his character which must be carefully noted.

As we have seen in Chapter 1, it needs to be emphasized that, though disobedient, Jonah is a believer in God. This is underlined by the confession he makes in 1:9, "I fear the Lord, the God of heaven, who made the sea and the dry land." Such a confession places him squarely in the mainstream of traditional Israelite beliefs (see Psalm 95:5). Even if this confession was forced out of him by the circumstances, there is no reason to consider it insincere or something learned by rote and repeated without conviction. This point of view is reinforced by the quotation of the ancient Israelite creed in 4:2 (see Exodus 34:6-7): "Thou art a gracious God and merciful, slow to anger, and abounding in steadfast love, and repentest of evil." This is an understanding of God which he "knows" (experiences at first hand) and affirms. Even though he wishes to limit God's exercise of these attributes, this is truly what he believes his God to be.

Jonah's piety also becomes evident in the fact that he prays (2:2, 4:2). 4:2 also implies that he prayed to God when the call to go to Nineveh originally came to him ("is not this what I said?"). Even if the prayer in 4:2-3 might appear somewhat abrasive in our eyes by the way in which Jonah approaches God, such honesty is typical of Israelite piety (see, e.g., Psalm 44:23ff.). Jonah is not dishonest or hypocritical. He tells it to God just as it is. He lets God know exactly what he is thinking. There is an openness with God here that is certainly commendable (not unlike Tevye in *Fiddler on the Roof*).

Moreover, in this situation, Jonah does take the trouble to pray. He doesn't ignore God. And, though his conflict is with God himself, he addresses himself to "the Lord." His prayer in 2:2 might be considered a "God of the gaps" kind of prayer (i.e., he prays only when he is beyond his own resources), yet again it is a typical response for an Israelite in the face of trouble.[2] And, if we include the psalm (see below, Chapter IV), the picture remains consistent. His Song of Thanksgiving is quite traditional in language and form, with the vows and sacrifices (2:9) an exemplary response for a faithful Israelite.

It is thus clear that Jonah is a believer. It is also clear that he is a disobedient believer. He flees from the task God calls him to. He remains stubborn and dogmatic regarding the position he has taken over against God. He becomes angry at God's gracious way of dealing with the Ninevites. He remains unrepentant regarding his sin throughout the entire book.

Jonah's attitude toward the heathen reveals similar positive and negative poles. It is striking how uncommunicative Jonah is in the presence of other people. In Chapter 1 he speaks only in verses 9 and 12, and in Chapters 3 only in verse 4. While speaking only when the situation dictates that he do so, he does confess his faith to the heathen sailors in 1:9 and offers a way out of the distressful situation for the sailors by offering to be thrown into the sea in 1:12. Thus it cannot be said that his attitude toward the heathen is unequivocally hostile.

But, while his attitude toward the sailors is basically positive, his stance over against the Ninevites is entirely different. He does not want to preach to them in the first place. When he finally does go, it seems to be with considerable reluctance (see below, Chapter VIII). When the Ninevites are not destroyed, he displays considerable anger, and remains unreconciled to their deliverance throughout the remainder of the book.

Now, if Jonah's attitude toward the heathen has both its negative and positive aspects, this means that his reluctance and anger regarding the Ninevites is not because they are heathen (or non-Jews). As we have seen, Jonah's problem regarding the Ninevites is their wickedness (1:2). Jonah's problem is that God is being too lenient toward those who are guilty, more particularly, toward those whose guilt is so overwhelming that it would be unjust to let them go scot-free. On the other hand, God's own people are suffering, and commonly at the hands of wicked people like the Ninevites. For Jonah, then, God's ways of dealing with his own people seemed to be at odds with the opportunities here being offered to the most wicked of heathen nations. This is simply not being fair!

Now if God cannot relate his response to human conduct in ways that conform to proper canons of fairness and justice, then what difference does faith in him make after all? As the people put it in Malachi 3:14f., "It is vain to serve God. What is the good of our keeping his charge or of walking in mourning before the Lord of hosts? Henceforth we deem the arrogant blessed. Evildoers not only prosper but when *they* put God to the test *they* escape." Their complaint would also be much like that reflected in Malachi 2:17: "Everyone who does evil is good in the sight of the Lord, and he delights in them. Where is the God of justice?"

In the light of these remarks we need to return to the characterization of Jonah which the book offers us. It is common to consider self-confidence, even pride, as characteristic of this audience. A closer look at certain actions and attitudes of Jonah, however, calls for some re-assessment at this point.

Just look at this list: flight, complaint, frustration, stubbornness, self-pity, sharp and mercurial anger, repeated and strenuous wish for death. Such a list does not at all suggest that Jonah is self-confident. In fact, self-pity would seem to preclude self-confidence. Moreover, the stubbornness and dogmatism that we see in Jonah seem to reveal a certain *lack* of self-confidence. He seems to have lost some of his equilibrium. Life is not at all going the way it should, and a certain insecurity seems to have overwhelmed him, erupting in unusual forms of behavior. In fact, things have deteriorated to the point that life seems no longer worth living.

All of this suggests an audience which is experiencing real hardship, whose life has not been particularly favored with blessing. It suggests an audience that has begun to raise serious questions about God's ways of dealing with the world, and more particularly, his chosen people. God seems to be looking with favor upon the wicked because they are prospering, and he seems to have turned away from his own people because their life is filled with difficulties. Or, to put it in the language of the book, God delivers the wicked Ninevites from their deserved judgment, but he won't let his people enjoy the small comforts offered by the shade of a little bush (see 4:6-8).

The Historical Setting

In view of this characterization, is it possible to determine when the book may have been written?

It is common for scholars to date Jonah 100-250 years after the return of the Jews from exile in Babylon (beginning in 538 B.C.).[3] While no single piece of evidence can demonstrate this beyond doubt, this general period probably is correct, though we suggest here a somewhat earlier time than do most scholars.

In support of this in a more general way, one may cite the following: the language used is more characteristic of the post-exilic period than of any other (a few words are never used in pre-exilic literature). Moreover, apparently unclear information about the city of Nineveh (see Chapter V) suggests a time when the city was no longer in existence (it was destroyed in 612 B.C.). Also, the world of thought in which the book moves seems most closely paralleled by other literature from this period or by problems known to be current to the Israelite community of this period.

We would like to explore this last point in greater detail. It has been most common to consider the book of Jonah as a reaction to the reforms of Ezra and Nehemiah (approximately 450-400 B.C.).[4] These leaders of the post-exilic community faced a number of problems associated with what might be called religious identity. This was associated in large part with the infiltration of pagan or semi-pagan religious ideas and practices into the community. This led Ezra and Nehemiah to take some rather decisive measures to cut the Jewish community off from non-Jews. However noble their intention, this move had rather unfortunate side effects. A separatist tendency developed that led to measures and attitudes of intolerance toward non-Jews and an exclusivistic perspective on the part of the Jewish community. It is thought by many scholars that this was the setting to which the book of Jonah was addressed. The author thus seeks to show the ingrown community that God's mercy was not simply intended for them but reaches out to include the entire world. (For a similar suggestion involving "prophets of salvation," see Chapter III below.)

There are, however, some difficulties with this point of view.[5] None of the specific issues dealt with by Ezra and Nehemiah are even alluded to in the book (such as mixed marriages and mixed languages, see Nehemiah 9, 10; Ezra 9, 10). Moreover, the primary issue facing the community was not a sharp conflict between Jews and everyone who wasn't a Jew in some universalistic sense, but between Jews and non-Jews among whom they lived (particularly Samaritans).

It would appear that we would be better served if we looked for a setting prior to rather than in reaction to that of Ezra and Nehemiah. Such a setting may well be reflected in the book of Malachi, a book probably written in the period 475-450 B.C.

The time of Malachi has been characterized as an age of spiritual depression.[6] The previous two generations had returned from Babylon full of hopes about the future. The prophets had built up these hopes through their announcements regarding the great future God had in store for them (see Isaiah 40-66; Joel 3). But now the better part of a century had passed and there was no sign at all that these prophecies were being fulfilled.

Life back home in Palestine was just as difficult as it had ever been, if not more so. The small community, consisting only of Jerusalem and its immediate environs, was under the thumb of foreign powers (Persia). The people were experiencing hardships at the hands of surrounding peoples such as the Samaritans and the Edomites. All were having difficulty ekeing out a life that could hardly in any sense be considered blessed. A general atmosphere of discouragement prevailed in the community.

This had its effect upon the religious life of the people. Not only did a kind of nonchalance come to prevail regarding more specifically religious duties (see Malachi 1:6-2:9, 3:7-10; Nehemiah 13:15-22), but there was also a breakdown in public and private morality (see Malachi 2:13-16, 3:5).

A basic cynicism regarding the Word of God had emerged. As in the time of Ezekiel (12:22-28, 18:25), the people of Israel believed that the "days grow long and every vision (of the prophet) comes to nothing." God's word was not trustworthy. They came to believe that it no longer needed to be honored or obeyed.

No doubt even those who remained faithful were beginning to ask the question: "If God loves us, where is the evidence that this is so?" (a paraphrase of Malachi 1:2; cf. Isaiah 40:25-26).

Why does he not demonstrate this to us through a fulfillment of the prophetic word? Why are we languishing under the heels of other people and suffering in ways that they don't? "Evildoers not only prosper, but when they put God to the test, they escape" (Malachi 3:15). In fact, it appears sometimes as if "everyone who does evil is good in the sight of the Lord, and he delights in them" (Malachi 2:17). If God is truly a just God, he should see to it that the rewards for faith in him and for living an upright life are distributed in a more equitable way.

Given this sort of situation, what difference does the life of faith make after all? Of what use are the special sacrifices of faith? Where does it get us? "It is vain to serve God! What is the good of our keeping his charge or walking before the Lord of Hosts?" (Malachi 3:14). Hence the nonchalance regarding religious life to which we have made reference above.

But such a crisis may lead to an even greater dismay. If the God upon whom you have pinned all your hopes disappoints you . . . ! If you have given your life over to God and there are no evident benefits issuing from that commitment . . . ! If God seems rather to be extending that blessing to others in a way unrelated to their faith or daily conduct . . . ! And then if you who have had your hopes dashed are asked to go and offer those same hopes to others who have obviously trampled all over God's law . . . ! Then, indeed, you, like Jonah, may just decide that life is futile after all and that with such a God as your God, death is to be preferred.

Such would seem to be a characterization of the audience to which the book of Jonah is addressed. Jonah is both subject and object of the book. The book was written not only about Jonah but for him.[7]

Notes

1. See H. W. Wolff, *Studien zum Jonabuch,* pp. 48-54, 72-3.

2. Over one-third of the Psalter consists of prayers spoken in this kind of situation, e.g., Psalms 3-7.

3. E.g., M. Burrows, "The Literary Category of the Book of Jonah," in *Translating and Understanding the Old Testament,* p. 105.

4. *Ibid.*

5. See R. Clements, "The Purpose of the Book of Jonah," *Supplements to Vetus Testamentum,* 28 (1975), pp. 16-28.

6. See John Bright, *A History of Israel,* SCM, 1960, p. 362.

7. See my "Jonah and Theodicy." H. W. Wolff in his commentary on Jonah (soon to be published) has now sketched a somewhat similar setting for the book, though dating it some 150 years later (the last third of the fourth century B.C.). I have been unable to consider his arguments but this date seems too late. Was it possible for a book to achieve canonical status among the prophets in a little over 100 years (i.e., by 200 B.C., see Eccles. 49:10)?

III

THE
IMPORTANCE
OF A WORD

Among the various literary devices used by the author, one of the most important is the repetition of key words.[1] The author thereby intends to draw the readers' attention to them. He calls the reader to study them with special care. It is unfortunate that the reader of the English Bible is not always able to perceive these repetitions. The reason for this is that the translators have not always used the same English word in translating the Hebrew.

Proper Names

Proper names are used so rarely in the book, it is almost as if the author wanted to use only those that were absolutely necessary. Whether you think the book is historical or not, you have to wonder why only Jonah is named among the various persons introduced in the story. And as for the places, it seems somewhat strange that only Nineveh, Tarshish and Joppa are mentioned (and the last two only in 1:3 and 4:2). Thus, inasmuch as the author normally chooses to omit names, he must attach some special significance to those he does introduce.

Tarshish is repeated three times in 1:3 and once in 4:2 (see Chapter VI for the arrangement of the words in 1:3). Though its site is uncertain, Tarshish is commonly located in present-day Spain. It was almost certainly chosen by the author (or Jonah) because it lay in the direction exactly opposite from that of Nineveh, and was the farthest known point in that westerly direction. The city may also have been chosen because of its symbolic value as a distant paradise (see 1 Kings 10:22; Ezekiel 27:12).

Joppa (1:3), the chief Mediterranean port (modern Jaffa) serving Jerusalem in the Old Testament period (see 2 Chronicles 2:16), serves the important function of placing the beginning of the story in Palestine, and not in some never-never land. This makes it clear that the story is about an Israelite, not about any man, nor about "every man." Also, it enables one to determine Jonah's geographical relationship to Tarshish and Nineveh.

Nineveh was the capital of Assyria for the last one hundred years or so of its life. Assyria had been responsible for some of Israel's greatest disasters. The northern kingdom was so totally destroyed in 721 B.C. that its tribes disappeared from history (see 2 Kings 17). In the years following, Assyria devastated the southern kingdom, Judah; it was miraculously saved only in the final hour (see 2 Kings 19).

Assyria thus remained the object of contempt in Israel's eyes for generations. Nineveh became a symbol of violence and oppression. The entire prophecy of Nahum, delivered sometime shortly before Nineveh's downfall in 612 B.C., gives a picture of this city in the eyes of Israel. Nahum does not spare the language, calling Nineveh the bloody city, full of lies, booty and dead bodies without end, a city that could be likened to a shapely harlot out to seduce all nations (3:1-4; see Zephaniah 2:13-15).

This picture of Nineveh was transmitted through the generations. When combined with the purposeful use of exaggeration in connection with Nineveh (see below, Chapter IV), its symbolic function in the book is clear. It is a symbol for the worst in the pagan world. Through his use of Nineveh the author almost seems to say: If the message that Jonah was to bring could have an effect upon Nineveh, it could have an effect upon anybody. But more than that, as we have seen, he uses Nineveh to raise sharply the question of justice. Nineveh had taken up the sword and should perish by the sword. But now Nineveh was to be offered the chance to escape the guillotine. Israel, God's covenant people, had had its head tumble from the block and now the executioner was being offered a new life! This was not a just way for the God of Israel to proceed.

As we have seen (Chapter I above), Nineveh is not a symbol for the heathen per se. Yet its value as a symbol for highlighting the relationship between the Jews and those to whom God's Word is to be extended must not be discounted. If God is concerned that his Word be heard in Nineveh, of all places, he must care enough about his world to want it to be heard everywhere. Nineveh thus serves to open up the world to Jews entrusted with the Word of God.

Jonah, son of Amittai. The reference to Jonah's father makes it certain that he is to be identified with the prophet mentioned in 2 Kings 14:25. Various reasons have been given as to why the author used Jonah as the subject for his book.

As we shall see (Chapter V below), it is possible that the author retold an existing story about a trip to Nineveh by the prophet Jonah. Yet the question remains as to why the author would have used a story about Jonah rather than some other person to speak a message to his generation.

It has been suggested that Jonah was chosen to be the central figure of the book because he gave voice to an Israelite nationalism.[2] Jonah was a "prophet of salvation," whose prophecies regarding Jeroboam's kingdom were highly optimistic (see 2 Kings 14:25). They would thus stand in contrast to the critical prophecies of his somewhat later contemporary Amos (see 6:13-14, 7:11). In using the traditional figure of Jonah, it is thought that the author thereby intends to criticize indirectly the prophets of salvation of his own day (see Joel 3:1-21; Isaiah 63:1-6; cf. Isaiah

34:1-17). These prophecies tended to exalt the place of Israel in God's future at the expense of all the other nations of the world. The author of Jonah thus condemns a religio-national pride in some of his contemporaries.

This interpretation fails to recognize a number of matters, however. The complete absence of any reference to prophecy in the book (see Chapter II above) should make one hesitant in saying that a fundamentally prophetic conflict is being addressed. Moreover, such an understanding assumes a reasonably secure people, confident that all will be well with their future (see Amos 5:18-20). But we have seen (Chapter II above) that the book reveals an audience *lacking* in self-confidence, quite uncertain about what God has in store for them. The book thus addresses those for whom such optimistic prophecies had seemingly *failed*. Also, we have seen (Chapter I above) that there is no radical Israel/heathen dichotomy in the book.

Finally, this perspective fails to see that the interpretation of Jonah's prophecy in 2 Kings 14 is a highly positive one. There is, moreover, no comparable evidence that his prophetic work in the time of Jeroboam was given a negative assessment. It is thus probable that the author uses the figure of Jonah in the positive sense represented in 2 Kings 14:24-27. The highly compassionate activity of God toward Israel (14:26) and his refusal to blot out Israel's name (14:27) in spite of Israel's persistent sinfulness (14:24) indicates clearly that God has had a *more than just* pity for *Israel* in the past. If God had dealt with Israel as she had deserved to be dealt with, she would have perished long ago (see Isaiah 48:9).[3]

The author's use of Jonah as the focal point for his message to his people would thus have served to recall this picture of God's gracious dealings with Israel in the past. The point for his audience would thus have been clear: If God has been more than just with Israel in the past, Israel (Jonah) should be able to understand God's dealings with the Ninevites more clearly than she has. God relates himself to people in ways that go beyond any simple system of justice. And he expects Israel to do the same. Sharpening this reason for choosing the figure of Jonah is the fact that Jonah was a prophet from the northern kingdom, Israel. Israel was destroyed by Assyria, whose capital was Nineveh, less than fifty years after Jonah's prophetic career (in 721 B.C.). Now, from the perspective of a later generation, it was seen that Jonah, who had announced the greatness of Israel's future under Jeroboam II, was called upon to offer a future to the very country that was later to put an end to Israel. As we have seen, how can God be just, if he offers life to the wicked Ninevites, when he had destroyed Israel (which was certainly no more wicked!)? Was not God being inconsistent?

These factors would seem to be sufficient reason for the choice of Jonah (and possibly, a story about Jonah) to speak to a generation like the one we have described (see above, Chapter II).

Finally, it has been suggested that the meaning of the Hebrew names Jonah and Amittai may have been important for the author.[4] Amittai means "truthfulness" or "faithfulness." An ironic point may be intended. Jonah as the son of truth abandons his faithfulness again and again.

Jonah means "dove," a metaphor sometimes used for Israel in the Old Testament (see Hosea 7:11, 11:11; Psalm 74:19). Thus Jonah = dove = Israel. This may have been a way for the author to make more transparent the fact that Jonah represents Israel as a whole and is not simply to be considered an isolated individual (see above, Chapter II).

Repetition of Key Words

Now we must look at other words which are repeated in the book.

1. *Great.* This is the most repeated word in the book (fourteen times). It occurs only twenty-eight times in the other eleven minor prophets. As we will see, the use of the extraordinary serves the author's use of irony well (see Chapter IV). Great is used six

times of Nineveh or the Ninevites (1:2, 3:2, 3, 5, 7, 4:11). The word is used to specify the great area and population of the city (3:3 even intensifies it, "an *exceedingly* great city" or, literally, "great even for God") and the extent of the response to Jonah's message. This great city is evil (1:2). Yet, even though great, Jonah hardly begins his work (3:2-3) and the city wholeheartedly responds to his message, including even the greatest (3:5, 7). Finally, the city in its greatness is stated as the object of God's pity (4:11).

The point made seems to be clear. It is no small hamlet that has responded to Jonah's message. In spite of the prophet's reluctance a great metropolis has been converted. How surprising, and how in contrast to Israel's own response! Yet, what a responsibility God's people have in the face of such potential.

But, however important the human factor is in bringing the message, such results are possible finally only because of the greatness of God's activity. Four times the word is used to refer to the means God uses to carry out his purposes (1:4a, 4b, 12, 17): wind, storm and fish. In addition to Nineveh such action had brought about a great response on the part of the sailors (1:10, 16).

But unlike both the sailors and Nineveh, Jonah's response in the face of this work of God is great anger (4:1). A response of great joy is possible for Jonah only when he himself experiences deliverance (4:6). God's goal for Jonah was to broaden that great joy so that it would be his response, not simply to the deliverance of the wicked Ninevites, but to all of God's actions on behalf of his creatures, no matter how unjust they may appear in the light of ordinary human considerations.

2. *Evil.* This word (noun and verb) occurs ten times in the course of the narrative (1:2, 7, 8, 3:8, 10a, 10b, 4:1a, 1b, 2, 6). It is used in two closely related senses. On the one hand it refers to the wickedness of people, the Ninevites (1:2, 3:8, 10) and Jonah (4:6). On the other hand, it refers to the judgment which is (is

not) visited upon human sinfulness by God (4:2), on Jonah and the sailors (1:7, 8) and on Nineveh (3:10).

Evil is here seen as a continuum (as in the Old Testament generally) whereby human wickedness sets into motion a chain reaction that leads *inevitably* to the judgment (like a pebble thrown into the water, whose ripples finally reach the shore), *unless* God intervenes. God can choose to break into this continuum (4:2) and not allow the judgment to take place. This is what he does for both Jonah and the Ninevites. (It is to be noted that the wickedness of the sailors is never mentioned. They suffer the evil of the storm because of *Jonah's* wickedness.) In the case of Jonah, his disobedience led to the evil of the storm, which God stopped before it achieved its destructive ends. In the case of the Ninevites, their wickedness led to the announcement of judgment, which God stopped because of their repentance.

In spite of Jonah's own deliverance, it is because of the latter intervention of God that Jonah reacts so violently in 4:1, literally translated, "And it was evil to Jonah, a great evil." This is the only time in the entire book that the word "great" is attached to evil. Given our discussion above, this means that the author is giving special attention to Jonah's reaction to God's repentance of evil. Jonah is here placing *God's* action under judgment! God's repenting of evil, his *saving* action, is seen by Jonah to be a great evil. This is an astounding judgment: Salvation is evil! Jonah has set himself up as judge over God. He is placing God's actions toward Nineveh under condemnation.

Now the final use of "evil" in the book (4:6) comes into focus. God comes to Jonah in order to save him from his evil (see below, Chapter IX). God's actions toward Jonah now become directed toward the deliverance of Jonah in the same way in which they were earlier directed toward the deliverance of Nineveh. Jonah is now where Nineveh was, only his wickedness is related to his judgment of God's actions. God in his gracious way seeks to move Jonah to repentance with a graciousness that goes beyond justice. Hopefully Jonah can see this and draw the proper conclusions regarding God's deliverance of the (now) Jonah-like Ninevites.

It is the evil in Nineveh and Jonah that prompts much of God's activity in the book. This divine activity is highlighted by the repetition of three words:

3. *Hurl.* In 1:4 God hurls a wind upon the sea. This action of God sets into motion all of the events of the first chapter, stressed by the repetition of the word "hurl." The sailors throw the cargo of the ship into the sea in order to appease the one who caused the storm (1:5) and finally Jonah (1:15), after Jonah himself suggests this measure in a sacrificial move (1:12). (For the significance of sacrifice in 1:12, see below, Chapter VI).

4. *Appoint.* God appoints a fish (1:17), a plant (4:6), a worm (4:7) and a wind (4:8). The degree to which God makes use of elements of the natural order to carry out his purposes is made strikingly clear here. They are used both as instruments of judgment (worm, wind) and of salvation (fish, plant).

And yet the book makes quite clear that such hurling and appointing on God's part is insufficient for the ultimate salvific purposes he has in mind for his creatures. He needs human beings to interpret the meaning of such natural occurrences (as in the case of the sailors) or to verbalize the meaning of such natural occurrences himself (as in the case of Jonah).

5. *Call.* This word occurs nine times in the book (including the related noun, "message," in 3:2). It is used primarily in two different senses. Four times it has reference to the proclamation of God's word to Nineveh (1:2, 3:2, 4). God's action thus takes both verbal and nonverbal forms. Four times it is used of the human cry to God in time of distress: Jonah (1:6, 2:2), the sailors (1:14) and the Ninevites (3:8). (It is also used once for the proclamation of a fast in 3:5, a response to the call of God.) All of the participants in the story, Jonah as well as the heathen, are placed on the same level of need before God in the time of distress. The call to God makes the difference between life and

death—for one and all. There is no difference among them in their need for deliverance from the hand of God.

This word, which has reference both to God's action and human response, provides a point of transition to words repeated to stress the human response to the activity of God. Some are positive and some are negative.

6. *Fear*. This word (verb/noun) occurs six times in the first chapter with some differences in meaning. The sailors react in fright to the storm (1:5). Then, in reaction to Jonah's confession that he fears the Lord (1:9), the sailors respond in "great fear" (1:10). Finally, after the stilling of the storm, the sailors fear the Lord with a great fear (1:16). In the last two instances both the verb and the noun are used together to intensify the reaction of the sailors. The sequence of events, triggered by God's action and furthered by Jonah's action in verses 9 and 12, leads the sailors from simple fright, to awe at the awareness of being in the presence of such a great God, to trust in the Lord. The movement is striking: from fear, to *great* fear, to great fear *of the Lord*.

7. *Turn, repent*. While "fear" is the word governing the rhythm of divine action and human response in Chapter 1, "turn, repent" translate a Hebrew word which is used five times to describe much the same rhythm in Chapter 3. The Ninevites turn from their wicked way (3:8) in the hope that God may change his mind and turn from his anger (3:9). When God sees that the Ninevites have turned (repented), he repents or relents (3:10). God's repentance is a sovereign, free response to the repentance of the people. In 4:2 Jonah confesses that this is indeed a characteristic of his God, a characteristic with which he is not altogether happy. It is the indiscriminate exercise of this repenting activity of God which occasions his conflict with God (see Chapter I).

8. *Go down*. While Jonah's response to the Word of God should have been an "arising" to go (1:2-3, 3:2-3, cf. 1:6), he chooses to flee initially, which leads to a progressive "descent." He goes down to Joppa (1:2), goes down to (on board) the ship (1:2), goes down into the innermost parts of the ship (1:5), and

finally descends to the very realm of death, Sheol (2:6). Down, down, down . . . the inevitable path of one who seeks to move in disobedient directions from the Word of God. This is clearly intended to depict a movement toward death (see Psalm 88:4-6; Proverbs 5:5).

9. *Anger*. While flight and descent are descriptive of Jonah's response in Chapters 1 and 2, anger characterizes his response to God's action in Chapter 4. One word for "anger" occurs four times with reference to Jonah (4:1, 4, 9a, 9b) and another word occurs twice with reference to God (3:9, 4:2). Jonah's anger is a response to God's slowness to anger (4:2), the turning away of his wrath (3:9). For Jonah in 4:4, God was not angry when he should have been angry. Jonah in his anger believes himself to be responding rightly to the situation. He decides that he will be what God should have been. He will be just if God will not be. This is a judgment on Jonah's part of God's non-anger.

Then in 4:9 Jonah is angry, not because God turned away his wrath, but because God *exercised* his wrath and visited destruction upon *Jonah* through the removal of the plant and its shade. Again Jonah by his angry response challenges the rightness of God's action. Only this time it relates to God's judgment rather than his deliverance. The issue here shifts to a sphere broader than the deliverance of Nineveh; it now includes God's actions toward Jonah (Israel). And Jonah's anger to the point of death is expressed so sharply here because he believes he perceives injustice in God's ways of dealing with him as over against Nineveh. The one he delivers, the other he judges. In the face of such unfairness, anger is the only appropriate response.

10. *Perish, die*. The human reactions we have seen are fundamentally related to the question of life and death. This issue is particularly focused in the use of these two words. "Perish" occurs four times (1:6, 14, 3:9, 4:10) while "die" (verb/noun) occurs four times (4:3, 8b, 8c, 9). It is also a prominent theme in the psalm in Chapter 2.

The captain (1:6), the sailors (1:14) and the king of Nineveh

(3:9) all pray for life in the face of the threat of death. When, however, the Ninevites are spared from death, Jonah expresses the wish to die (4:3). On the other hand, when Jonah's own plant is *not* spared (4:10), he expresses the wish to die even more strenuously (4:8f.).

The issue at stake for Jonah is thus the question of life and death. God and he disagree as to who should live and who should die. God has the unjust continuing to live and the just experiencing death. If this is the way things are to be, then life is absurd. Death is much to be preferred to life with a God such as this. Or, in the remarkably parallel words of Socrates, "If the rulers of the universe do not prefer the just man to the unjust, it is better to die than to live."

11. *Pity*. This verb is used twice, in 4:10-11. When used of human beings, it has reference to the actions of a ruler (1 Samuel 24:11; Psalm 72:13; Jeremiah 21:7), or a representative thereof in instances of war (Deuteronomy 7:16; Isaiah 13:18) or administration of justice (Deuteronomy 13:9, 19:13, 21, 25:12). Thus there is a sovereign decision or action in view when this verb is used. It characterizes a movement from a superior to those who are subordinate in some way. It relates to superiors who are (are not) moved to pity toward those who are within their jurisdiction. Clearly implicit throughout the usage of this term is the right of the sovereign (or his representative) to have pity or not have pity as he sees fit in specific circumstances of life.

This verb thus does not have reference to some fixed attribute of God such as, e.g., love. An abstract statement about God's compassion for his creatures cannot be inferred from these final verses in Jonah. There is, in fact, frequent reference to God's *refusal* to exercise pity (see Jeremiah 13:14, 21:7; Ezekiel 5:11, 7:4, 9). God does not always act in a pitying fashion. The basic idea of the verb is much less that of a subjective "compassion" than of an objective "sparing," though the two ideas might be brought together to give the sense in 4:11: may God not be "moved to spare" Nineveh.

In context, then, the verb "pity" has reference to a sovereign's right to act in a pitying manner toward others in particular situations (see below, Chapter IX).

Notes

1. Wolff, pp. 36-40, to which we are especially indebted.
2. *Ibid.,* pp. 14-16.
3. See my "Jonah and Theodicy," pp. 227f.
4. G. Knight, pp. 56-58. Yet Israel is not alone in being called a "dove" (see Jer. 48:28). Cf. Allen, p. 181.

IV

IRONY,
STRUCTURE
AND UNITY

The Irony of Jonah

Recent studies of Jonah have shown that the book is filled with irony.[1] The recognition of the ironical elements is very important for properly understanding the book. First of all, it is necessary to make clear what irony is, and then certain guidelines for the interpretation of the book can be made.

In the most basic sense, irony is a figure of speech in which (a) the intended meaning is the opposite of that which is stated, e.g., referring to a palace as a humble home, or (b) an event, statement, etc. occurs or is used in a way just the opposite of what is expected, e.g., a lifeguard drowns or a Christian bombs a church.

Irony is generally used in literature as a vehicle for criticism. It serves to point up inconsistencies, incongruities in a situation between what is and what ought to be. As such, irony is commonly used by those who wish to state a truth to those who are guilty of prostituting it in some way. Irony will hold up their shortcomings to reprobation by various means: ridicule, absurdity, burlesque, exaggeration, humor, or other ways of intensifying incongruities. This is normally done for the purpose of provoking change, to redeem the situation rather than simply to condemn it. Irony is also characterized by understatement or suggestion rather than plain statement, leaving the burden of recognition and the drawing of the moral to the reader (thus risking the failure of recognition).

Now if Jonah is pervaded by the ironic, as we shall see, then this should have the following implications for any interpretation of the book:

1. Jonah is criticism. The author seeks to expose some departure from the truth in the audience to which he addresses himself. Yet Jonah is *constructive* criticism. The word "polemic" is probably too strong to describe the book, for the author is not merely opposed to something. He protests in the sense of seeking to bring about reform or change in the lives of his readers. Jonah witnesses to the truth. Thus the book not only criticizes, but makes some positive declarations about the matter under discussion.

2. Variety in ironic presentation should be expected, such as ridicule, exaggeration and even more subtle incongruities of one kind or another. Thus anyone who would not consider the book a unity (see below) must work with special care, for incongruities are the very stuff out of which the book is created. Moreover, the use of understatement in irony must alert us for understandings not always evident in the surface meaning of the text, especially since the author's work would have been subtle even for the original readers of the book. Thus it will be easy to "under-interpret" the book.

3. The recognition of irony in the book will affect one's understanding of the type of literature to which Jonah belongs (see below, Chapter V). While virtually any type of literature may use irony, the pervasiveness of it in Jonah would seem to delimit the possibilities sharply. The common designations of parable or short story (or even a historical account) would need to be further defined by the words ironical or satirical.

Here are some representative examples of the irony in the book (leaving others for inclusion in Chapters VI to IX).

1. One group of ironic thrusts relates to what one expects of a prophet of God (or faithful Israelite) and what one actually encounters in his speech and actions. Sometimes this is set over against the conduct of the heathen that would be exemplary even for a faithful Israelite.

    a) Jonah abandons the task to which he is called.

    b) Jonah sleeps during the storm while the heathen pray.

    c) The pagan captain has to plead with Jonah to pray.

    d) Jonah remains unrepentant, despite continuous divine efforts, while the heathen respond to God with relatively little provocation.

    e) Jonah's anger over the conversion of Nineveh. Jonah's wrath occurs at precisely the point where God turns his wrath away.

    f) The heathen's openness to the sovereignty of God stands in contrast to Jonah's closed-mindedness (cf. 1:14, 3:9).

    g) Jonah does not wish to give God opportunity to be true to himself (4:2).

2. Another set of ironic points relates to incongruities in Jonah's actions in their relationship to each other, as well as in relationship to the results one would expect from his actions.

    a) Jonah flees from God's call, yet confesses him as Lord (1:9).

    b) Jonah recognizes that God sent the storm because of his guilty behavior (1:12), yet this issues in no repentance on his part.

    c) Jonah's overwhelming success in such a wicked city and with such meager efforts.

    d) Jonah's joy over the gift of (extra!) shade in the midst of his twice-expressed wish for death.

    e) Jonah's joy over his own deliverance and his anger over Nineveh's deliverance.

    f) Jonah's wish for death upon his success.

    g) Jonah's anger to the point of death over the destruction of such an unimportant bush.

3. Elements of exaggeration heighten the irony of the book throughout (see the use of "great" in Chapter III above).

    a) The size of Nineveh (see below, Chapter V), the breadth and instantaneousness of the conversion, including the involvement of animals in the process of repentance. The author deliberately overdraws these scenes in order to highlight the irony of the prophet's totally unexpected success. He, of course, intends the success to surprise his readers. They would have remembered the earlier prophets like Jeremiah who vainly attempted to reach the people with the Word of God (and Israelites at that!).

    b) Jonah's being swallowed by and surviving in a fish, and the plant's quickly growing and dying. This serves to highlight the troubles God has with his own people in contrast to that of the Ninevites. All those miracles and yet they were unrepentant!

4. Finally, we must take a more concentrated look at the psalm in this light (2:2-9; see below, Chapter VII).[2] The psalm, a song of thanksgiving, is sung by Jonah in gratitude to God for sending the fish to save him from drowning in the sea. As such, it has an ironic relationship to the surrounding narrative as a whole and in its details.

Jonah's reaction of praise and thanksgiving for *his own* deliverance (very similar to 4:6) stands in sharp contrast to his reaction to the deliverance of Nineveh. God's deliverance extended to Jonah in spite of his *lack* of repentance (both in Chapter 2 and in 4:6) would be denied by Jonah to the Ninevites who have in fact repented. The one with whom God has been *more than just* insists that God treat the Ninevites according to their *just* desserts! Moreover, Jonah's confession at the climax of the psalm (2:9), "Deliverance belongs to the Lord," stands in sharp incongruity to the limitation which Jonah places on that deliverance when it comes to Nineveh.

In the details of the psalm, the ironic thrust is also strong. Jonah contrasts himself with those who have "forsaken" (!) their true loyalty (2:8b) and worship idols (2:8a). Note the emphatic "But I" in 2:9. Jonah fled to get away from the Word of the Lord (1:3) and yet incongruously turns to that Lord for action when the going gets rough (2:4b, 7). He offers his life (1:12) and yet prays desperately for life when confronted with the actual realities of death in the sea (a similar incongruous juxtaposition of life and death-wish in Jonah is seen in 4:6, 8).

It is thus striking the degree to which the psalm participates in the irony of the rest of the book, and may in fact heighten that irony in significant ways.

The Structure of Jonah

The biblical writers speak not only by means of the words which they use, but also in the way they order those words. They convey ideas not only through what they say, but how they shape what they say.

Structures seem to be very important to the author of Jonah as well. At the beginning of each of the expositional chapters (VI-IX) we will suggest possibilities for the structures found within them. In addition to searching for such internal structures, one must also ask about the way in which the author has outlined the book as a whole.

It would appear that the following outline best reflects the development of the thought of the author:[3]

   a) 1:1-3   Introduction
   b) 1:4-16   Focus on the sailors
   c) 1:17-2:10   Focus on Jonah
   d) 3:1-3a   Recapitulation of the introduction
   e) 3:3b-10   Focus on Nineveh
   f) 4:1-11   Focus on Jonah

The basic pattern of the four main sections (see below) suggests that (a) and (d) must be set aside by themselves as being introductory in character. 1:1-3 serves to set the stage for all that follows.[4] It sets up the problem that the book will pursue, namely, the conflict between God and Jonah over his preaching to the wicked Ninevites. Moreover, the basic characters of the book are noted: the Ninevites, the sailors (through reference to the ship), Jonah and God.

3:1-3a is virtually identical to 1:1-3 and essentially serves as an introduction to the second half of the book. The task of going to Nineveh is once again given to Jonah. This time he goes.

The other four sections are virtually self-contained cameos. They are quite sharply delineated from one another both in terms of their natural movement and in terms of the character concentration. 1:4-16 concentrates on the sailors, and the entire incident is never referred to in the book again. 1:17-2:10 concentrates on Jonah and, again, the details are not even alluded to in the last half of the book. The concentration of 3:3b-10 is on Nineveh, while 4:1-11 returns to focus upon Jonah. Neither of the latter two sections is anticipated in the former two major segments of the book. With the interchange of a concentration upon heathen and Jonah, the book as a whole assumes an ABCABC pattern.

Also characteristic of each section is the movement from a crisis to a (attempted) resolution of the crisis. Basic to this movement is a pattern of human response to divine action and divine response to human action. The book has a fundamental concern with sketching the ways in which both heathen and Jonah (Israel) respond to God's activity (in both creation and redemption). At the same time, it betrays a special interest in demonstrating the responsiveness of God to the varieties of human reaction to what he has done. God is revealed as one who is persistent while at the same time being remarkably open to change.

God is the one who initiates the crisis in each of the sections. He throws the storm (1:4), he throws Jonah into the sea (2:3, cf. 1:15), he sends the word of judgment to Nineveh (3:4) and he delivers the city (3:10).

Varieties of human response then follow. In the first section, the sailors react with fright, worship of their own gods, inquiries, awe, physical labor and prayer to Yahweh, the God of Israel. Interwoven with these are the reactions of Jonah in verses 9 and 12 (see below, Chapter VI). In the second section, Jonah reacts with prayers (see 2:2). In the third section, Nineveh responds with faith and rites of repentance. In the fourth section, Jonah reacts with anger, complaint and a wish for death (4:1-3).

Varieties of divine response now follow. He delivers from the storm (1:15), from the sea (2:6b) and the fish (2:10), and from destruction (3:10). In the final section he responds to Jonah with a question (4:4).

Finally, there are varieties of human response to God's actions, all of which were merciful. The sailors worship Yahweh (1:16), and Jonah sings a Song of Thanks and vows to worship Yahweh in the same way (2:9). In the final section, however, Jonah reacts with obstinacy (4:5). This triggers the final conversation between God and Jonah (4:6-11).

In drawing out some of the implications of this analysis,[5] we see that in the first two sections there are no significant differences between the pagan sailors and Jonah with respect to their beseeching God, the deliverance they receive from him, and the type of response they make to the source of their deliverance. The point made seems to be clear: the sincere cry to God is efficacious whether it comes from a pagan polytheist or from one of God's own prophets. There is no difference; God extends his love and mercy to all who call upon him.

In the last two sections there are important differences between the pagans and Jonah. Here the pagans come off better in the comparison. They are more responsive to the call of God than Jonah is. How much more trouble God has with his own people than with the worst of the heathen world!

In the two sections devoted to Jonah some very interesting

incongruities are noted. The one focuses on Jonah's own deliverance, the other focuses on Jonah's reaction to someone else's deliverance. Jonah is joyful when he is spared and angry when Nineveh is. There is revealed here the heart of the argument between God and Jonah: *Who* is to be the object of God's deliverance?

In the two sections devoted to the pagans there are some important similarities as well as differences. Both reveal that the heathen are "willing and able" to respond to the call of God. Yet they respond in ways that are different. Our word studies have shown (see above, Chapter III) that certain words prevail in describing the sailors (fear, hurl), while others describe the Ninevites (turn, repent, also believe). It is striking, too, that the name of God is different in these sections (the Lord in the first, God in the second). This may well suggest that God responds positively to different kinds of human response. Contrary to a perspective that appears to be held by Jonah, God has more than one way of relating to his people.

This structure thus assists us in isolating key aspects of the book's message.

The Unity of Jonah

Finally, we must briefly bring together some considerations that bear on the question of the unity of the book. Is the book as we now have it the product of a single author, written as a unified whole? Most scholars have answered this in the negative.[6] They believe that the psalm is a later addition to the book, perhaps by an editor who wished to make Jonah into a rather more pious individual.

We believe these scholars to be mistaken. The psalm appears to fit into the book very well indeed. We will list here the major objections to the unity of the book, together with replies.[7]

1. The psalm is a Song of Thanksgiving (see below, Chapter VII) and seems singularly inappropriate in the mouth of one

who has just been swallowed by a fish. (This, of course, simply transfers the problem to the redactor or editor.) One has to be careful about drawing negative conclusions from unusual occurrences in this book! It seems clear that Jonah sings his thanksgiving because he has just been saved from drowning. As we shall see (Chapter VII below), the fish is viewed as a vehicle of God's deliverance.

2. The picture of a thankful Jonah seems at odds with the picture we get of him in the rest of the book. Yet, as we have seen (see above, Chapters I and II), this is precisely the picture of Jonah the author wishes to present to us. Jonah is a man of faith engaged in a theological conflict with his God. This means that Jonah is a divided man. He can clearly reflect the faith that is his, and yet remain adamant in his convictions regarding the matter at issue between God and himself. This will be particularly the case when God acts graciously on his behalf (as in 4:6).[8]

3. The vocabulary, style and theme of the psalm are quite different from the prose sections. This is certainly due in part to the fact that the author used already existing psalm materials to compose the Song (see below, Chapter VII). Because it is poetry, the style would obviously be different.[9] There is a rather small overlap of vocabulary (call, go down, sea, sacrifice, vows, steadfast love). Yet it is striking that, as we have seen above and in Chapter III, there are also quite different usages of vocabulary between Chapter 1 and Chapters 3 and 4.

As for themes held in common, there is much more similarity at this point than is generally recognized. The references to the sea (the storm is over, hence reference to it would not be appropriate) connect the psalm well with Chapter 1. The psalm is fully suited to Jonah's situation. The strong interest in death relates it well with all chapters (see above, Chapter III). We have seen above that the themes of crisis, crying for help and deliverance are common to all chapters. The references to worship life (2:4, 7, 9) are also quite prevalent in the surrounding narrative (see 1:5, 7, 14, 16, 3:5, 6, 7, 8). Verbal images used (even with different vocabulary) are also quite common (e.g., casting, forsaking, presence of God, distressful cries, hearing and answering). Given the relatively self-contained scenes of the book (e.g., 1:4-16 is never referred to in Chapters 3 and 4) one should expect something similar when it comes to the psalm.

The striking place irony plays in the psalm (see above) as well as the way it fits into the structure of the book also support the integrity of the psalm in the book. One might also add that the typical character of the psalm (see Chapter VII) fits well with the typical character of the book as a whole (see Chapter II).

It thus seems probable that the author of Chapters 1, 3 and 4 composed a psalm out of traditional poetic materials and used it for his particular purposes. It is possible that it was an already existing psalm, otherwise lost, but the overwhelming amount of imagery related to the sea suggests that it was put together especially for usage in this context.

Notes

1. E. M. Good, *Irony in the Old Testament*, pp. 39-55, M. Burrows, pp. 80-107. See also Wolff's commentary on Jonah.
2. Cf. Good, p. 54.
3. Cf. W. Rudolph, *Joel-Amos-Obadja-Jona*, 1971, p. 326.
4. Wolff, p. 54.
5. Cf. G. Landes, "The Kerygma of the Book of Jonah," *Interpretation*, 28 (1967), pp. 26-27.
6. E.g., J. Smart, "The Book of Jonah," in *Interpreter's Bible*, volume VI, 1956, p. 874. So also now Wolff's commentary on Jonah.
7. See especially Landes, *passim*.
8. The verb used for "pray" in 2:1 is rarely used for Songs of Thanksgiving (e.g., 1 Samuel 2:1), but there is no indication that it is a word used only by redactors. Here the verb is structurally parallel to its usage in 4:2.
9. Yet, there is evidence of a similarity of style at one point. The narrative device of delaying notice on certain matters (e.g., 1:5b, 10b, 4:2) is also present here, with the reference back to what happened to Jonah when he was in the sea (1:15).

V

FACT

OR

FICTION?

For over two thousand years most Christians and Jews have viewed the Book of Jonah as a historical narrative. (An early dissenter was Gregory of Nazianzus, fourth century.) It has been considered a reliable account of some rather extraordinary happenings in the life of one of God's own prophets. There has emerged in more recent centuries, however, a perspective which views the book as essentially different from a historical account. Those who maintain this position understand the book to be more like the parables of Jesus than the books of Kings. Who is right?

The answer is not easy to come by, and no final solution is possible which absolutely excludes the other alternative. Whatever decision one makes on this question, it must be remembered that what is most important is enabling the *message* of the book to be heard clearly. It is commonly thought that if one has been convinced of the story's historicity (or non-historicity), then one has somehow heard its message. But the question of "happenedness" is only preliminary to a discernment of the message of the book.

It should also be remembered that the decision on the question of happenedness is not necessarily connected to the question of the truth of the narrative. Imaginative types of literature, such as parables or short stories, are just as capable of speaking the truth of God's Word as any historical narrative. The fact that Jesus in his teaching used such literature more than any other single type to do just that, should assist us in thinking about this matter.

We should also indicate that the book *is* historical at least in the sense in which it reflects the life and thought of the Jewish community.

The following paragraphs seek to lay out the kinds of questions that one must ask in considering this matter. It will become evident that we believe that there is a balance of probability in favor of seeing the book more in terms of Jesus' parables than in terms of 2 Kings.

On the one hand, there are some pieces of evidence that point in the direction of the historicity of what the book reports. 2 Kings 14:25 refers to a prophet named Jonah from the town of Gath-hepher, near Nazareth. He lived during the reign of Jeroboam II, king of Israel (786-746 B.C.), and prophesied regarding the extent of Jeroboam's kingdom. He would thus be a virtual contemporary of Amos.

This must be taken with full seriousness. Yet it needs also to be remembered that there are other examples of Jewish literature where a historical figure is used as a basis for imaginative literature (e.g., see the additions to the book of Esther and Daniel, included in the Roman Catholic Old Testament). Thus it is possible that the author used the figure of Jonah in this way (for some suggestions as to why he did this, see above, Chapter III). In any case, the reference to 2 Kings does not *necessarily* mean Jonah is a historical narrative.

Sometimes an appeal is made to Jesus' use of Jonah (Matthew 12:39-41, 16:4; Luke 11:29-32). Does not this indicate that the book is a historical narrative? This, however, is no certain clue regarding the question we are raising. Jesus may have referred to Jonah in much of the same way that a modern preacher might refer to incidents from the parables of Jesus, e.g., the merciful deeds of the Good Samaritan. If Jesus had made reference to the parable of Jotham in Judges 9, that certainly would not commit us to understand that story as historical narrative. Jonah, the fish and the men of Nineveh may well have served as types for him, as, e.g., the Prodigal Son does for us today. Thus the appeal to Jesus cannot be used as evidence in deciding the historical question.

On the other hand, there are certain aspects of the book that make it difficult to accept as historical material.

One of the more common elements isolated is the series of improbable occurrences in the story. One has to be careful here. In assessing the reasonableness of such matters the possibility of miracle must always be kept in mind. At the same time, one has to beware of making the jump from what God *could* have done to what he actually *did* do. Of course God could have accomplished such things. The question, however, is, given the evidence at our disposal, did he in fact do these things?

We are assisted in this matter in some ways by the presence of some improbable occurrences in which God was not involved. This, in turn, raises questions about the character of the book as a whole. It turns out that the story of the fish is not nearly the problem that some other matters are.

It is thus improbable that the beasts of Nineveh fasted, cried out mightily to God and turned from their wicked ways (3:8). It is improbable that Jonah would have prayed a Song of *Thanksgiving* for having been delivered while in the belly of the fish (2:2-9). It is improbable that a city with hundreds of thousands of people hostile to Israel and Israel's God, would have been instantaneously and completely (without exception!) converted. One might even ask, from what we know about the relationship between God and human beings elsewhere in the Bible (and from two thousand years of church history!), whether such an occurrence is not impossible.

The latter is made even more improbable by the fact that such an event did not leave its mark anywhere else in recorded history. The Assyrian archives from the eighth century have been discovered.[1] They refer to a solar eclipse, a famine, a pestilence, internal corruption and military disaster, but there is no evidence of a conversion. Moreover, no trace of such an event was left in the subsequent history of the empire. Records show that the goddess Ishtar and other deities were worshipped in Nineveh down to its fall in 612 B.C. Assyrian warfare was as violent as ever through these years, though Jonah 3 specifically reports a turning away from such conduct. An especial instance of such violence was the campaign of devastation in Israel, Jonah's homeland. Perhaps within the very lifetime of Jonah himself Israel was completely destroyed by these people (see 2 Kings 17). If one should suggest that the conversion was so superficial that it didn't deserve further mention, or had little effect, then the point of the book of Jonah is blunted, for the conversion is represented as being so sincere that God abandoned all intention of destroying the city.

In the light of improbabilities such as these, one is given to wonder whether other matters in the book ought not be considered in the same way. While there are fish with large enough gullets to swallow Jonah whole (e.g., the sperm whale), the problem is that he emerged some seventy-two hours later from the mix of digestive juices completely unscathed. That a plant could grow large enough to provide shade in one day is also improbable. That God *could* have made provision for such is absolutely necessary for the understanding of the book, for the author does involve God at these latter points. But the question is whether, in the light of the other improbabilities noted, another explanation might be more in order.

We have noted (Chapter IV above) that exaggeration is one of the ways in which an author can speak ironically. It seems probable that the above aspects of the story are to be explained in this light. They serve to intensify incongruities in relationship to Jonah's thought and action. The exaggerations are used by the author to make his points in an especially sharp way. This is especially so in regard to what the author says about Nineveh. In every conceivable way he exaggerates its greatness. Six times he uses the key adjective "great" to describe the city or its inhabitants (see Chapter III). He speaks of it as a city "three days' journey in breadth" (3:3). This would involve a distance of some fifty to sixty miles. Archaeology has shown that the city was nowhere near this large (a diameter of about three miles). Such an exaggeration may also be the case with reference to the population of 120,000 very young children in 4:11. This would probably mean a total population of one million or so, five times or so more than the known population of the city.

Whatever may have been the author's actual state of knowledge about Nineveh (e.g., we know that Nineveh did not become the capital or chief city of Assyria until after the time of Jeroboam II, and that referring to "the king of Nineveh" is like referring to the king of Oslo), it is probable that the author in most of these instances is exaggerating to make his point rather than lacking in information.

If most, if not all, of these references to Nineveh are correctly interpreted as purposeful exaggerations, then the improbable events of which we have spoken above fall right into place. The city, mammoth in area and population, extraordinarily wicked in all of its dealings, experiences a total conversion, extending even to the cows and the chickens!

The point of the exaggeration seems twofold (see Chapter VIII): (a) It stresses the potential effect that the preaching of the Word of God has and thus, indirectly, the responsibility of those who are called to see that it is articulated. (b) It highlights the difficulty that God has had with his own people.

The latter point is made chiefly in connection with Jonah's more personal experiences, and this through the use of purposeful exaggeration as well. Oh, what troubles God has had with his people! And in such contrast to the Ninevites (see Ezekeiel

3:4-7). Not one spokesman for God, but many of them and for so many years. And more than prophets! Storms at sea, and miraculous rides home in fish and sheltering gifts, unexpected and undeserved. All that divine activity, all those miracles, and look at the response. "The men of Nineveh will arise in the judgment with this generation and condemn it" (Matthew 12:41).

It is thus not enough finally to pass off these improbable elements in the story as evidence for its unhistorical character, and leave it at that. Purposefully formulated, they contribute in significant ways to the shaping of the message of the book. Yet, recognized as ironic exaggerations, these elements serve to reinforce the judgment that the book is not intended to report on historical events. This ironic cast, this intensification of incongruities, that pervades the book, suggests that the author's *intention* moves beyond any simple reporting of events in the life of Jonah and others.

There are two further factors that can be drawn upon to assist us in discussing our question regarding historicity. One, the carefully worked out structures in the book (see Chapter IV and the beginning of Chapters VI and IX) suggest a non-historical intention on the author's part. Such a concern for structure and symmetry is not as characteristic of straightforward historical writing and is more suggestive of an imaginative product.

Two, the pervasiveness of the didactic element in the book suggests a similar conclusion. Virtually every phrase in the book is intended to teach. The kerygmatic and theological possibilities in every verse far exceed that which is to be found in other historical narratives in the Old Testament (e.g., 2 Kings). The abrupt ending, which makes an appeal to the reader rather than informing us about Jonah, betrays this central concern of the author.

A final reminder on this point is in order. To consider the book something other than historical literature does not detract one whit from its religious or theological value. Both the Old Testament and the New Testament use parables and other types of imaginative literature (e.g., Judges 9:7-15; Isaiah 5:1-7) in addressing a word of God to his people. There is no *necessary* relationship between the truth of a narrative and its historicity. Jesus' parables are no less true because they did not happen. And so, whatever one's decision on the question of historicity, the book of Jonah is true. So we *believe*.

If the evidence pushes the balance of probability clearly in the direction of imaginative literature rather than historical narrative, we need to inquire as to what kind of imaginative literature it is.

It is often noted that Jonah bears some striking resemblances to the story of Elijah and Elisha (e.g., 1 Kings 17-19) and should therefore be considered a story of the same type, i.e., a story about a prophet. As our exposition will show, there are clear points of contact between Jonah and these stories about prophets, not only in detail (cf. 1:1 with 1 Kings 17:8f.) but also in theme (e.g., the miraculous element).

There are, however, too many differences to consider Jonah simply a story parallel to those of Elijah and Elisha. Unlike the latter, the didactic element in Jonah is very pervasive, emerging in virtually every sentence. Also, unlike these stories, Jonah is anything but a heroic figure. He is in fact an anti-hero. That is, he is the leading character, but lacks those attributes that make for a figure of heroic proportions. Unlike the other prophets, Jonah is not the one who performs wonders; God is.

There are, in fact, some indications in the book which suggest that Jonah may have been sketched so as to serve as a *contrast* to Elijah (see the exposition on 4:3). Yet, it is striking the degree to which Jonah *as a prophet* remains hidden in the book. As we have seen (Chapter II above), he is nowhere called a prophet, nor is the prophetic office much on display. The emphasis in the book is clearly not on what God is doing for others through the prophet, but on the struggle between God and Jonah himself. Nevertheless, and this constitutes yet another difference, the

Book of Jonah is clearly a prophetic word in a way that the stories *about* the prophets are not.

There are some scholars, however, who think that Jonah was misplaced when it was included among the twelve minor prophets.[2] They think that the book is not prophetic literature in any proper sense. We must disagree with such a perspective.

It is true that Jonah is unique among the prophetic books in many respects. It contains only five words (eight in English) of prophetic oracle (3:4). Moreover, it consists *completely* of a story about a prophet. Third person narratives do occur in other prophetic books, but nowhere near the proportion we find in Jonah (and elsewhere they occur chiefly in the service of the oracles accompanying them). Also, Jonah is the only prophetic book which was written for an Israelite audience where no claim is made that a word from God has been received for this purpose. A word from God is received by Jonah, and eventually delivered, but it is a word intended for Nineveh, and *not* for the audience to which the book as a whole is addressed, namely, the people of Israel. Sometimes it is stated that Jonah is distinct among the prophets in that no specific historical situation is in obvious view. But that is also the case with prophetic books like Joel and Obadiah.

Nevertheless, we think that Jonah's placement among the prophetic books is quite justifiable. This was recognized already by the year 200 B.C. (Ecclesiasticus 49:10).

With regard to type of literature, Jonah is not absolutely unique among the prophets. It *is* strikingly different from the earlier prophets such as Amos and Hosea. But as the history of prophetic literature shows, increasingly complex types of literature are used by them. This is so largely because of the changing historical circumstances into which the prophetic word is spoken. Thus we find that parables, allegories and other narrative materials are used by the prophets (see Isaiah 5:1-7; Ezekiel 1-7, 23; cf. 2 Samuel 12:1-6). Thus, while no other prophetic book has a type of literature exactly like Jonah, there are sufficient examples of a prophetic message taking story form so that Jonah is not unique at this point.

There are also literary similarities between Jonah and other prophetic literature at one other point. The use of the question in Jonah plays a role not unlike that of the Book of Malachi. For example, every statement directed to Jonah includes a question. This suggests an audience where dialog between people and prophet is one of the common forms of discourse among them. It is probable that the increasing difficulty which prophecy faced in the post-exilic period (see Psalm 74; Zechariah 13) necessitated radical changes in the form of prophetic proclamation (Malachi and Jonah also are similar in terms of content, as we have seen in Chapter II above.)

Another point of contact between Jonah and the other prophets is that Jonah consists of a critique of the people. The book aims at amendment in the lives of those to whom it is directed (see above, Chapter IV).

Finally, it might be noted that the symbolic value of Jonah's activity is parallel to the symbolic actions of other prophets (see Isaiah 20; Ezekiel 4:1-15) in some ways.[3] What the prophet *does* rather than what he says becomes a vehicle for the Word of God.

Jonah's placement among the prophets thus seems to have been a fundamentally sound decision by the later Jewish community. They seem to have recognized that the form which prophetic literature takes must be related to changes in the community to which it is addressed.

Yet we are still left with the question of what type of literature the prophet used in this book.

Jonah has been considered an allegory.[4] An allegory is a type of literature in which the main terms of the text have a hidden or figurative meaning (see Isaiah 5:1-7, where verse seven explains the hidden meanings; Ecclesiastes 12; Ezekiel 15).

The center of the allegorical interpretation has been the big fish. With reference to Jeremiah 51:34, 44, which use the imagery of being swallowed by a sea monster to speak of Israel's being sent into Babylonian exile, it is suggested that the picture of Jonah being swallowed by the fish is a metaphor for that historical event. Then, Israel like Jonah turned to God while in captivity (three days and three nights), and having been spewed out back to her homeland again, she begins to take up the task of proclaiming the faith to the nations.

There are, however, major problems with this way of interpreting the book. The passages in Jeremiah refer to a sea monster and not simply to a fish (as in Jonah). The fish in Jonah is viewed as an instrument of salvation, not of judgment (which Babylon was). Moreover, the fish receives much too much attention in this interpretation for the small part it actually plays in the book. Finally, other allegories in the Old Testament follow interpretive patterns which can be discerned by all in their broad outlines. Such is not the case in Jonah, where so much material does not lend itself to an allegorical interpretation and, where attempted, brings little agreement among interpreters.

There is a sense, as we have seen in Chapter II, where Jonah may be said to represent Israel or some group within Israel, but the book cannot be considered a figurative account of her historical experiences.

Jonah has also commonly been designated a parable.[5] A parable, so familiar to us from the Gospels, is an extended simile or metaphor and (unlike the allegory) uses words literally. As a very general designation this might be satisfactorily used in connection with Jonah. Yet its starting point with a historical personage, the didactic force behind so many of the details of the story, and the direct way it speaks of God's presence and action suggests that this designation is not as exact as it should be.

Some scholars have recently taken to calling Jonah a satire, given the significant role that irony has in the book (see above, Chapter IV).[6] I think this is correct as far as it goes. So many different types of literature, however, can be used to speak satirically (e.g., an essay or an editorial). Thus satire is probably not precise enough, yet the ironic character of the book necessitates that we describe it as satirical literature.

Other scholars prefer to call it simply a short story, noting the narrative art in particular.[7] It is thus commonly compared to Esther, Daniel 1-6, and especially Ruth. There are few characters and their traits are left undescribed in any explicit sense. Character is revealed more through concentration upon the action of the story rather than through thoughts noted and speeches given. The scenes are highly concentrated, and tend to be self-contained cameos. Throughout there are elements of suspense and excitement, yet there is no explicit statement drawing a moral. Nowhere does the author say: This is the point I am trying to make. The story is told in such a way that the readers would have been able to identify themselves with the main character (see above, Chapter II). Yet Jonah is so clearly an Israelite, and so many of the events are so extraordinary (and hence atypical), that it falls short of being an "everyman" type of story.

There remains one major drawback to the simple identification of the book as a short story. The didactic element is so pervasive. All the way along the story line the author's pedagogical interests arise, albeit in an indirect fashion.

Finally, we might note that there are elements in the story that have prompted some to call the book a myth or a fable. The participation of animals in rites of repentance, as well as making fish, worms and plants important "characters" in the story suggests what one commonly finds in fables. Also, certain fairy tale motifs seem present in the intermingling of human beings and animals, Jonah and the fish in particular. There are many stories from both the ancient and more modern world that have motifs parallel to those in Jonah (e.g., Pinocchio). Nevertheless, it must be said that, while the author may indeed have borrowed such motifs from the surrounding cultures, he has shaped the material in such a way that something quite different emerges upon any comparison with these folkloristic parallels. There is no known parallel where the varieties of material we have in Jonah are brought together in a similar way.

Perhaps the best we can do is call it a satirical, didactic (or theological) short story.[8] It has no exact counterpart in the Old Testament or in known literature from the ancient Near East. All suggestions at present must thus remain somewhat on the speculative side. Nevertheless, there is some value in the kind of exercise in which we have engaged in this chapter, because it enables us to say with some probability what the book is *not*. In any case, what is important in such study in the end is whether it has contributed to elucidating the *message* of the book.

Notes

1. A. Parrot, *Nineveh and the Old Testament*, 1952.

2. Smart, p. 871.

3. See J. McGowan, "Jonah," in *The Jerome Bible Commentary*, 1968, p. 634.

4. G. A. Smith, *The Book of the Twelve Prophets*, volume II, 1898, pp. 502ff.

5. Smart, p. 872. So also now Allen, pp. 175-181.

6. Burrows, p. 96.

7. Wolff, pp. 33-34.

8. H. W. Wolff in his commentary on Jonah has now taken a similar position. The sometimes suggested category, midrash (an edifying exposition of a Scriptural text), seems unlikely because no single text is in view. See Allen, p. 180.

VI

THE

SUCCESSFUL

ESCAPE

Jonah 1:1-16

Initially we must take note of the way in which the author has ordered his material in this first chapter. We have seen (Chapter IV) that after an introduction focusing on God and Jonah (1:1-3), the center of attention shifts basically to the inter-relationships between God, the sailors and Jonah, with a general pattern of crisis (1:4), human response (1:5-14), divine response (1:15), and human response (1:16). Verses 4-16, however, seem to have been ordered according to a more detailed ABCCBA chiasmus:

A. Narrative Framework (4-5a)

   1. God hurls a wind and the storm starts (4).

   2. Sailors fear, cry to their gods and sacrifice to them (5a).

A¹. Narrative Framework (15-16)

   1. Sailors hurl Jonah and the storm stops (15).

   2. Sailors fear Yahweh, speak their vows and sacrifice to him (16).

73

B. Narrative/Request (5b-6)

1. Jonah sleeps deeply in the face of the storm (5b).

2. Captain requests Jonah to pray to his God so that they do not perish (6a).

3. Captain professes sovereign freedom of God (6b).

C. Dialog (7-9)

1. Sailors speak to one another to determine who has done wrong (7a).

2. Report—Jonah is revealed by lot (7b).

3. Sailors request information from Jonah (8).

4. Jonah responds — I fear (9).

B¹. Narrative/Request (13-14)

1. Sailors strive to bring ship to land (13).

2. Sailors pray to Jonah's God so that they do not perish (14a).

3. Sailors profess sovereign freedom of God (14b).

C¹. Dialog (10-12)

1. Sailors speak to Jonah to determine what he has done wrong (10a).

2. Report — Jonah's wrong is revealed (10b).

3. Sailors request information from Jonah (11).

4. Jonah responds—I know (12).

The following summary observations may be offered regarding this structure:

1. Parallels in corresponding lines may be observed in each instance at the level of both content and form. In terms of content the lines are usually either synonymous (e.g., verses 6b, 14b) or antithetical (e.g., verses 4, 15). The antithetical parallels serve chiefly to contrast the conduct of the sailors and Jonah (e.g., verses 5b, 13) or to highlight the change in the sailors (e.g., verses 5a, 16). In terms of form, parallels are exact throughout (e.g., question is parallel to question).

2. The corresponding lines exhibit differences as well as similarities. By this means the author makes a point or heightens an effect. Thus in verses 11, 13 the repetition of the phrase concern-

ing the tempestuous sea serves to do the latter. The author expands upon the parallel in verse 10 in order to emphasize the increased fear of the sailors, while he does the same in verses 12, 14 in order to say something important about life and death.

3. This structure helps explain some unusual stylistic features of the chapter. Thus the somewhat abrupt transition at points (e.g., between verses 6 and 7) can be explained in terms of an interest in achieving these parallels. Also, the delayed notices in the chapter (verses 5b, 10b) may also have resulted from this interest.

4. In the final (climactic) lines of each of the major sections a significant point is reached which the author wishes to emphasize.

    a) Sections A, A^1 (verses 5a, 16). Here the difference in the sailors' response to God's action is noted. The repetition of the word "fear" (see above, Chapter III) spotlights that reaction and, because the word is used in different senses, highlights the difference in that reaction. They have moved from sheer fright to trust in the Lord. They have shifted from the worship of their own gods to the worship of Yahweh, the God of Israel.

    b) Sections B, B^1 (verses 6b, 14b). One of the major theological motifs of the book is highlighted here (see below, Chapter VIII): the sovereign freedom of God to respond to situations as he wills. It is ironic, of course, that such a mature theological insight is spoken by the heathen rather than by Jonah. Jonah's conflict with God revolves around this very issue.

    c) Sections C, C^1 (verses 9, 12). These are the only statements of Jonah in the chapter and provide the only clue to the status of Jonah's continuing conflict with his God. While these statements are in effect challenges of God as we shall see, they witness both to the importance of Jonah in accomplishing the work of God as well as to God's ability to make use of even such disobedient ones to accomplish his purposes.

Jonah Rises . . . and Runs

The opening phrase of the book, "Now the word of the Lord came . . . ," is identical to that which is commonly found elsewhere as an introduction to a prophetic book (see Hosea 1:1; Joel 1:1). The command that is given ("Arise, go") is, however, paralleled only in the Elijah-Elisha narratives (see 1 Kings 17:9, 21:18). Here is a tie to Elijah to which the author will return (see below, Chapter IX).

While the book opens as a typical book by a prophet, it immediately becomes something quite different. The readers of the book, having read the first words, no doubt began to prepare themselves for something that they had heard before. A prophet is being called by God to get up and preach.

The surprise no doubt comes with the mention of Nineveh (verse 3). While prophets had commonly been called upon to speak against the nations (see Jeremiah 46-51, Ezekiel 25-32), no other prophet had been called upon to put in a personal appearance. To speak was one thing, to actually *go* there and deliver it was another.

The readers of the book would thus be immediately sympathetic with Jonah. If Jonah had been told to repeat what Nahum said, for example, then there would have been no problem. But to give Nineveh an opportunity to actually *hear* the word was to open up possibilities for a positive response from the city. And that was for Jonah (and for the readers of the book) an intolerable situation. Why? Because "their wickedness has come up before me" (1:2). On Nineveh, see above, Chapter III.

We are now face to face with the question: Why does Jonah flee? Simple answers will not suffice here. It is not because he is afraid (see 1 Kings 19:2-3; Jeremiah 26:21), or because he views the task as too difficult or beneath his dignity. He does not, like Moses or Jeremiah or Gideon (see Exodus 4:10; Jeremiah 1:6; Judges 6:15) flee because of some inadequacy he feels regarding his abilities to handle the situation. He does not raise questions because he thinks the message given him is too hard for the people to hear (see Jeremiah 20:9; Amos 7:1-6; Isaiah 6:11). Thus, while other prophets draw back at times from the task laid on them, and some flee out of fear, none seek to flee from "the presence of the Lord" and none flee for the reasons Jonah flees.[1] The reason is stated in 4:2.

It is striking that the giving of the actual reason is delayed until 4:2, almost the end of the book. This is not done simply to heighten the dramatic effect for the original readers. The reason was to obscure for the readers who were identifying themselves with Jonah what their *real* reasons for doing so were. They would perhaps not admit to the reasoning given in 4:2 initially. After all, you don't go around saying, or even admitting to yourself perhaps, that you don't like the fact that your God is merciful. The author thus holds back on the real reason until his audience is fully identified with Jonah and is brought along to the point where the truth of the matter can have its sharpest impact.

Jonah then flees because he fears that the people of Nineveh would repent and that God, being the gracious and merciful God that he is, would not destroy them after all.[2] (It is clear from "Is this not what I said" in 4:2 that God and Jonah had had no little discussion about the matter.) Jonah wanted no part in such an endeavor because the wickedness of the people had reached the point where God's judgment should just fall on them (see Psalm 139:19-22, 79:6). They should have no opportunity for a second chance as it were. How quickly and gladly Jonah would have gone if he could have been *certain* Nineveh would have been destroyed!

This relationship between wickedness and judgment was clearly the common understanding in Israel. Those who sin are to reap the inevitable consequences thereof (see Exodus 34:7). "He who digs a pit will fall into it" (Proverbs 26:27). Sin sets in motion consequences which snowball, only finally to fall back on those who committed the sin in the first place. This is the moral order of things established by God and, from Jonah's perspective, he should adhere to his own basic principles.

Thus, what it boils down to for Jonah is that God is too wishy-washy when it comes to dealing with the wicked. God is much too lenient a father toward the guilty. For Jonah, when you have a guilty people on your hands, when the wickedness has piled up, it is just not right to speak of slowness to anger (4:2) and alleviation of punishment. When the cup of wrath is full, God should give it to the wicked, not drink it down himself (see Joel 3:13; Jeremiah 25:15-38; Isaiah 10:12-19)! [3]

Thus, as we have seen (Chapter I), the basic conflict between God and Jonah becomes one of justice. God has poured out his wrath on Israel and upon Judah, and even now his people were having difficulty surviving. And God comes with a message which makes possible a way out of judgment for the most violent people in the world. Such a word has to be stilled forever.

It should be made clear that Jonah does *not* understand his rebellious reaction to this word of God to be a rejection of God himself. Jonah is not fleeing because he doesn't believe in God. As we have seen (Chapter I), the problem is basically a *conflict of beliefs* between God and Jonah. He is running away not because of *unbelief,* but because of a certain *belief* which he has.

This raises an important issue in the book, the possible conflict between beliefs and obedience. It is possible for the faithful to articulate their faith in such a way as to make it difficult, if not impossible, for them to respond in obedient action in certain situations. Beliefs, doctrines held dearly, can lead to disobedience. Theology, the articulation of the meaning of faith, and obedience are closely related to one another. Jonah is disobedient finally because his theology has gone bad at one point (see below, Chapter X).

This means, then, that the issue between God and Jonah is not basically one of obedience and disobedience. The issue is fundamentally a theological one, pertaining, as we have seen, to the justice of God in indiscriminately extending mercy. Jonah's disobedience is only a symptom of a more basic issue. Thus, in the interpretation of the book, we need to remember that it is not Jonah's faith which needs reviving so much as his theology which needs changing.

Running Away from God

Verse 3 seems too repetitive for a good author. Tarshish is mentioned three times and "away from the presence of the Lord" twice. This is due, however, to the structure chosen by the author, an ABCDCBA chiasmus.[4]

A.   To flee *Tarshish* from the *presence of the Lord.*

 B.   He *went down* to Joppa.

  C.   He found a *ship.*

   D.   Going to *Tarshish.*

  C.¹   He paid *its* fare.

 B.¹   He *went down* into the ship (i.e., on board).

A¹.   To go with them to *Tarshish* from the *presence of the Lord.*

The center point of the verse is going to Tarshish (repeated in opening and closing clauses). This serves to stress Jonah's travel in the direction completely opposite Nineveh (see Chapter III). His flight was thus not without considerable calculation. "From the presence of the Lord" is also a key phrase (see verse 10). One is tempted to say that Jonah's efforts to escape are surrounded by the presence of the Lord. But the phrase needs further study.

Upon receiving the call to go to Nineveh, Jonah is determined to flee from the presence of the Lord. Does he really believe he can do that?

It is necessary to distinguish between two types of God's presence in the Old Testament:[5] God's cultic presence (focused in

Israel's life of worship) and God's structural presence, his presence in the world as a whole. Israel believed that God had graciously condescended to make his dwelling place among them in a way he had not done for any other people (see Exodus 33:14-16). Thus, God's word was articulated and his will made known in Israel such as it was in no other place. As far as God's rule and power were concerned, however, that was believed to be worldwide (see the distinction made in Genesis 4:16; cf. 2 Kings 17:18, 24:20).

This is comparable to a contemporary understanding of God's presence. It is commonly believed that there are contexts where God's Word is heard in a way it is not anywhere else. The church community is believed to be such a place. It would thus be possible to speak today of fleeing from the Word of God in the sense of staying away from certain contexts where one knows such a word will be spoken.

Luther says something strikingly similar:

> It is therefore possible to flee from God in the sense that we may run off to a place where there is neither Word, faith, and Spirit nor the knowledge of God. In that way Jonah fled from the presence of the Lord, that is, he ran away from the people and the land of Judah, in which God's Word and Spirit and faith and knowledge were present. He fled to the sea among the Gentiles, where there was no faith, Word and Spirit of God.[6]

Thus when Jonah resolves to flee from the presence of the Lord, he is not intending to cut himself off completely from God. He is not seeking to remove himself to a world where God is, as it were, locked out. He knows there is no such place, as his confession in 1:9 indicates (see 1:12). Rather, Jonah decides to sever his connections with that context where God's word and will are clearly made known, namely Israel. He seeks a place, not where he would be removed from God's rule, but where he would not have to continue to hear that word of God's commissioning him to go to Nineveh. He seeks to get rid of that "chirping in his ears." [7] (Are there parallels to be drawn here with the flight of the Prodigal Son?)

Viewed from his perspective, Jonah's flight is not from God, but from the Word of God. More particularly, a flight from a particular articulation of that Word: Go to Nineveh. If, then, Jonah is all that the author believes some of his readers to be, these people have set their minds in such a way that it has become very difficult for them to hear the Word of God in all of its fullness. A belief they hold dear prevents them from hearing. In somewhat different words, the flight for them might be said to be a theological cop-out. It represents a hardening of belief, a refusal to hear another Word on the matter.

There is another nuance that may be present in this phrase. One statement used of the prophet (priest) is that he *"stands* in the presence of the Lord" (especially used with Elijah, see 1 Kings 17:1, 18:15; Jeremiah 15:19). This has reference to one's readiness to serve another (cf. 1 Kings 10:8). Jonah does not stand; he flees. Unlike Elijah he repudiates servanthood. Jonah's flight may thus be said to be a flight from the service of a God whose demands are to his mind unacceptable.[8]

It is just this action on Jonah's part which, when later explained to the sailors (see verse 10), strikes terror into their hearts. Hence the heathen sailors react to such behavior in a way that Jonah (Israel) should react.

It is sometimes suggested that Jonah was rather presumptuous in thinking that he could frustrate the purposes of God. Hardly. God needs people. That is, he has chosen to make himself dependent upon human beings in the carrying out of his purposes. Thus people like Jonah *can* frustrate God's work in the world. God's purposes will be accomplished, for he can bring good out of evil, but Jonah (and Israel) can make it a much more difficult matter.

The Inescapable God

In the rest of the chapter irony is especially evident (see above, Chapter IV). Jonah, in seeking to avoid the task of mission, ends up converting not only the Ninevites but the sailors, too. His flight is thus eminently successful, though not, of course, in the way that he had hoped.

In verse 4 God acts to prevent Jonah from completing his flight. As events unfold it becomes clear that God's purpose is finally not that of judging Jonah for his disobedience. He wants to bring him to the point not only where the call to go to Nineveh can be reconsidered, but also where the theological conflict can be settled.

God is the "Hound of Heaven." He does not simply allow Jonah to go his own way. He persists in seeking him out in hopes that he will come to his senses. Jonah may deserve simple punishment for what he has done. But simple justice is not God's way. His love drives him beyond justice. To the end of the book he pursues Jonah, taking the way of mercy.

Sometimes there has been a tendency to stress the power of God in these verses (as well as in the book as a whole). God can whip up a storm in a moment and then suddenly quiet it down. He can call on fish and worms (!) to do his bidding. He can cause plants to grow up in a day and wither as quickly. Superficially this would suggest that God has developed a stage-show designed to show all his muscle-power. In the face of this kind of display, Jonah and the others could only bow the knee in adoration.

But this would be to misunderstand. Of course God has all power at his command. But a sheer display of power in and of itself can never lead to faith and obedience (cf. Luke 16:30-31). In the face of inarticulate power, the sailors' reaction is sheer fright and a turning to *their own* gods (verse 5). (Though this verse is often interpreted to mean that they throw the cargo overboard to lighten the ship, it can mean that the cargo is a sacrifice to the gods in order that the *sea* might be lightened.) That the sailors eventually move to another kind of fear, the fear of Yahweh, is possible only because of Jonah's confession (see 1:9).

At the same time we must not over-react here. God's display of power has served an indispensable function. It has (in addition to stopping Jonah) captured the sailors' attention. It has communicated something. It has provided a context where the ears are more attentive than they would otherwise be. The sailors listened to Jonah with an earnestness and sensitivity that would not have been the case if the sea were calm and all was well.

The storm has also communicated something to Jonah. He infers that he is being punished by God by means of the storm (see verse 12). But the context out of which Jonah interprets the meaning of the storm is different from that of the sailors. Because of his faith in Yahweh, what happens in the natural order (here and elsewhere in the book) is somewhat more transparent to him. But it is by no means absolutely clear to Jonah either. The meaning of such powerful natural events is ambiguous, even to the person of faith. Yet such a person should be more open to perceiving God's actions in the inarticulate events of the world in which he lives.

The key to the effectiveness of such actions is having an articulate human interpreter, one who can place the event within a larger context of divine activity (like Moses at the Red Sea). Only then can it be seen (and even then only in a glass darkly) that the action is not whimsical or capricious, or a sheer display of power. It is a sovereign action of God designed to lead to ends that are consonant with his salvific purposes (see below, verse 9).

Irony becomes evident again here. The heathen respond in distress just as good Israelites would, praying and offering sacrifices. Jonah sleeps. The Hebrew word indicates it is a deep sleep, not the sleep of one who is fearful or whose conscience is disturbed (see Isaiah 29:10; Genesis 2:21). No tossing and turning here. Jonah is comfortable with the decision he has made. Luther calls it the "sleep of death" (cf. Psalm 88:4-6), saying, "There he lies and snores in his sins." [9]

Ironically, the captain has to wake him up and plead with him to pray. The pagan has to remind Jonah of his religious responsibilities! He realizes that it is the call to God which makes the difference between life and death (see above, Chapter III). Jonah's only response is silence. The silence of perseverance. He could just as well have stayed asleep.

While Jonah is silent, the captain articulates one of the key motifs of the book: "Perhaps the god will give a thought to us, that we do not perish" (1:6b, see 1:14b, 3:9). God will act as it pleases him, which may or may not conform to human patterns of action. God is inescapable, but also unsearchable. (For further discussion, see below, Chapter VIII).

God and Jonah Found Out

As was common in their world of thought, the sailors believed that the storm was the direct reaction of a god to some evil deed committed by someone on board. They thus move to find out who the culprit is. Perhaps he could fill them in on his religious beliefs to such an extent that they could find a way to appease the god and stop the storm.

So they cast lots. We don't know very much about lots and their usage in ancient Israel (and other countries). They are most commonly used in early Israel, but also appear in later times (see Acts 1:26). They were used in a variety of decision-making contexts, from discovery of a wrongdoer (see Joshua 7:14; 1 Samuel 14:36-42) to choosing a king (see 1 Samuel 10:20-21). It was believed that God would determine the way the lot would fall (probably something comparable to a throw of dice). The decision would thus be a divine one in the final analysis (see Proverbs 16:33). The lot thus becomes another example of the use which God makes of "things" in the accomplishment of his purposes.

The lot points to Jonah. [10] Jonah is "stormed" with questions as a consequence. It is difficult to correlate the questions asked in verse 8 with the answer of Jonah in verse 9. It is clear from verse 10, however, that Jonah had more to say to them than is reported. "I am a Hebrew" would probably supply enough of an answer for the last three questions. (The designation "Hebrew" is used almost exclusively when foreigners are addressed, as in Exodus 2:7, 3:18). The question, "What is your occupation?" may mean, "What are you doing on this ship?" (see Psalm 107:23). If so, Jonah informed them that he was fleeing from the presence of the Lord (as verse 10 reports). The sailors' questions to Jonah here anticipate God's questions to him in Chapter 4.

The center of Jonah's response, however, is his confession of God as Creator and Lord in verse 9. ("Fear" here denotes simply trust in God and the confession is probably a creedal phrase used in Israel's worship, cf. Psalm 95:5, 136:26.) Is Jonah sincere or not? Here he is, running away from the command of God, and he confesses, essentially, "I believe in God, the Father, Maker of heaven and earth." It is probable that Jonah here is no different from any other person of faith, confessing the faith in a context surrounded by disobedient actions of one kind or another. As we have seen, Jonah's problem is not that of faithlessness. It is a theological position that has led him into disobedience. He does trust in God. He does pray and recite the creeds as one who believes. But his theology, to say the least, needs a little work.

And Jonah is certainly not naive. As we have seen, he does not think he can run away from God himself. So Jonah can be perfectly consistent in making this confession about God as Creator and trying to flee from that context where God's will is made known in a preeminent way.

This verse functions in a number of ways in this chapter. As we have seen, it shows how indispensable Jonah is. It is only his articulation of the name of Yahweh that enables the sailors to move from simple fright to trust in Jonah's God. Only through him do they become aware of to whom to pray and whom to trust and worship. Thus, whatever Jonah's intention, it functions as a confession to the heathen sailors.

At the same time it tells us something about God. As sovereign Lord he is in control of the situation. He rules the sea and the dry land. It also tells us something about a God who is able to work through imperfect people to bring about good. The verse is probably also intended to say something to the readers about what their confession *could* accomplish. If Jonah, how much more those who are obedient to the command of God!

But this verse also needs to be seen in terms of the conflict between God and Jonah. The tone of his voice cannot be heard, but it was probably a frustrated confession thrown into the teeth of the howling storm. One can see the kinds of pressures that are brought to bear on Jonah before he speaks out. He is literally backed into a corner by the sailors through the fall of the lots and their pointed questions. He knows that the jig is up. His flight has been permanently interrupted, his plans are no longer viable and his life has been placed in utmost danger. A calm and detached statement seems most unlikely in view of these circumstances.

Verse 9 does make it clear what Jonah believes about God. He is sovereign over all creation. But there is perhaps a not so hidden question in his confession: What is God doing with all of his power? To what use does he put it in his sovereign rule of the world? Will he act in a capricious manner, or will he conform his actions to basic canons of justice? "Shall not the Judge of all the earth do right?" (Gen. 18:25).

Putting God in a Corner

The sailors' reaction to Jonah's confession is striking. They become "exceedingly afraid" (verse 10; on "fear," see above, Chapter III). Their question is at the same time an outcry: What is this you have done (see Genesis 3:13)?! They cannot quite imagine anyone treating their god in such a fashion. Here the pagan sailors are revealed as having a respect for the divine that Jonah does not have. They couldn't imagine themselves doing such a thing. At the same time it functions as a question, as they seek to have Jonah spell out the implications of his actions. They realize that Jonah is guilty and that he has yet to confess to God what he has done. We will see this same kind of insight on the part of the sailors in verse 13.

With the storm getting worse and worse, the sailors press Jonah for a solution (verse 11). They realize that he alone would know how to respond to his own God in such a situation.

It is now necessary to take a somewhat closer look at verse 12. It is one of the high points of the chapter. It reveals both the attitude of Jonah toward the sailors and the status of his continuing conflict with God.

It is possible that (with some scholars) one should understand this demand of Jonah as one final attempt on his part to flee from God—to flee into death. He would rather die than go to Nineveh.[11] Yet this interpretation seems unlikely, for (unlike 4:3, 8) Jonah's mood here gives no evidence of anger, depression or despair.

To begin with, it is striking the extent to which verse 12b is parallel to verse 7 (8a). These two lines serve to begin and end the dialog:

> know-because of whom-this-evil-upon us
> know-because of me-this-great tempest-upon you

Jonah here confesses that it is his action that has caused this evil to be visited upon the sailors. Jonah admits that he is the guilty one. The storm is the consequence of his behavior. He knows, then, that he stands under the judgment of God and that death is a probable result.

What can he do now? It is impossible for Jonah to persevere on this present course because the sailors are demanding that something be done. Thus in this situation there are only two things left for him to do.[12] He can repent. This he refuses to do.

If he had done so, the storm would have stopped and the sailors would have taken him home (as they try to do in verse 13). Jonah remains obstinate in the face of his knowledge that God is exacting judgment upon him. Thus, while he admits his guilt before the sailors, there is no sign whatsoever that he regrets his course of action and turns to God.

On the other hand, he can persist in his conflict with God. This he does by what amounts to a peremptory challenge. To see this it is necessary to note the close parallels between verse 12a and verse 5b:

Throw-the cargo-into the sea-make light-from upon them
Throw-me-into the sea-quiet down-from upon you

We have noted above the presence of the motif of sacrifice in verse 5. This motif is also present in this parallel. It may be stated as follows: Just as the sailors hurled their cargo into the sea as a sacrifice to appease their gods, so now Jonah offers himself as a sacrifice. But for what purpose? Two answers seem to be required:

1. A sacrifice for the sailors. Jonah is moved by the sailors' plight; his sense of justice will not allow the innocent to suffer for the guilty. He is here theologically consistent. This seems clear from the phrase, "then the sea will quiet down for you," which is expressly what they request from Jonah in verse 11. Jonah's giving of his life (though forced upon him by the circumstances) is a means by which the sailors are delivered from evil and eventually come to their fear of God in verse 15. This text shows that it is Jonah's understanding of justice that determines his stance toward the matter, and not a radical exclusivism over against the heathen per se. This answer is incomplete, however, because it leaves the theme of Jonah's confession of guilt without point in relationship to his unrepentant stance toward God.

2. A sacrifice to God. Jonah admits that he is guilty, yet he will not repent. And so he will satisfy God's justice! He will take upon himself what he deserves. He will appease God's wrath!

In a clever move Jonah has here succeeded in throwing the ball back into God's court. He will show God how to act justly. What will God do now?

As it turns out, God delivers Jonah. He refuses to take the cue from Jonah. He is more than just with him. He does not return evil for evil, but breaks through the scheme which says that all sinful acts must have their punishing consequences. God responds in merciful deliverance. This is the history of God with his people again and again. Yet, in spite of this, they react as Jonah does in Chapter 4.

The Sailors Change Gods

Verse 13 indicates again how sympathetically the author treats the sailors. While pressing Jonah hard by means of their questions, they handle him in a quite considerate manner. They do not immediately do what Jonah tells them to do. They seek to find a way out of the dilemma that will not entail sacrificing Jonah. This action also suggests some insight on their part into God's will for Jonah. The sailors seem to understand that it is not Jonah's death that is being demanded by God, but only that he be brought back to the place where his conflict with God may be resolved.

This positive portrayal of the heathen stands in contrast with the behavior of Jonah in the chapter. They have been drawn into a death-filled situation through no fault of their own by this Jonah and yet they seek to save him.

This is certainly intended to be a deliberate contrast to that set up in 1:1-3. There the Ninevites are the wicked ones and Jonah reacts strongly against any idea that they should be offered a chance to live. Now Jonah has been placed in a situation not unlike that of the Ninevites. He is doomed to die as a consequence of his wickedness. Yet the sailors try to save him! Would that Jonah were more like the sailors in his stance over against Nineveh!

Now the sailors pray to Jonah's God, the one responsible for the situation in which they find themselves. They want to make sure that Jonah's God understands what they are about to do. They impress upon him that *he* is responsible for these developments. They should not be punished for carrying out the will of God!

This prayer is a typical lament (see Psalm 86), with an invocation, petition in time of severe distress, and a statement of confidence in God. In many respects, they are praying the prayer that Jonah should be praying. Jonah does eventually pray a lament (see 4:2) but that stands in some contrast to the sailors'. Both prayers (1:14, 4:2) have the "life" of Jonah as their central concern. The sailors ask that Jonah's life not be the cause of their death, while Jonah asks that his life be taken. The sailors desire life. Jonah wants death. The sailors acknowledge that God does what he pleases (see Psalm 115:3, 135:6), while Jonah expresses his frustration because God does precisely that. (For the theme of God's freedom, see below, Chapter VIII.)

The phrase "innocent blood" in verse 14 does not mean that the sailors believe Jonah is innocent (cf. verse 10), but only that, if by some chance he is or that they are making the wrong move, they not be made responsible for what they are about to do (see Deuteronomy 21:8-9). The sailors want to be absolutely sure that they are fulfilling the will of God! How in contrast to Jonah!

The sailors throw Jonah into the sea (for key word "throw," see above, Chapter III). He now becomes the sacrifice (cf. verse 5). They thereby become active participants in the carrying out of the purposes of God. They become a link in the chain that leads to the conversion of Nineveh. The sea becomes quiet.

The response of the sailors is striking in its simplicity and overpowering in its implications. The use of the key word "fear" (see above, Chapter III) clearly indicates that the author wishes to speak of their conversion to Jonah's God. They are now at the point where they can confess what Jonah did in verse 9, though willingly and gladly and without question. The pattern of their response, so alike that of Israel's, shows that whatever is Israel's is freely available to the heathen.

All of this comes about finally through the power of God. But also a key aspect of the chapter, as we have seen, is that Jonah, though reluctant, provides an indispensable witness that enables this result to occur. It is difficult to avoid the conclusion that if God's people would only respond to his call to mediate the blessing they had received, this is but a foretaste of the response they would receive.

Notes

1. Wolff, pp. 19-20.

2. Luther, pp. 51-52.

3. Luecke, p. 8.

4. See N. Lohfink, "Jona ging zur Stadt hinaus (Jona 4, 5)," *Biblische Zeitschrift,* 5 (1961), pp. 185-203.

5. Landes, pp. 19-21.

6. Luther, p. 45.

7. See Wolf Mankowitz, "It Should Happen to a Dog," in *Religious Drama 3,* ed. M. Halverson, Meridian, 1959, pp. 121-135. This is a fine example of putting Jonah in the form of a play.

8. This is not an adequate understanding of the phrase in and of itself, however, because it doesn't explain the attempt to flee all the way to Tarshish.

9. Luther, pp. 57-58.

10. The restatement of the question of verse 7 in verse 8 probably indicates that the lot only pointed to Jonah as the source of information rather than as the one who was guilty. They now need more precise information from him. Cf. Allen, p. 209.

11. See E. Haller, *Die Erzählung von dem Propheten Jona,* 1958, p. 24.

12. Cf. Landes, p. 23; Allen, p. 211; A. J. Glaze Jr., "Jonah," *The Broadman Bible Commentary*, p. 164; T. S. Warshaw, "The Book of Jonah," *Literary Interpretations of Biblical Narratives,* p. 193.

VII

SAVED
BY
A FISH

Jonah 1:17—2:10

To begin with we must make some comments about structure. This section is bracketed by two similarly constructed lines that focus on God's activity:

The *Lord* appointed a great *fish* to swallow *Jonah* (1:17)

The *Lord* spoke to the *fish* and it vomited up *Jonah* (2:10)

This signals the fact that God's action is primary in this section. God is finally the one who is responsible for casting Jonah into the sea (2:3). He delivers Jonah from death by drowning (2:6) by means of the appointed fish (1:17), and then completes the deliverance by speaking to the fish and having it vomit up Jonah on dry land (2:10).

This relates to one of the major themes of the book. God has delivered Jonah quite apart from the question of justice. If one were to ask into Jonah's (Israel's) *just* reward, given his disobedience, then God should *not* have had pity. But God's saving action moves beyond the question of justice. The point made is clear: Israel has no right to raise the question of justice regarding Nineveh.

At the same time it is necessary to stress that Jonah's response is not unimportant here. Before each of the two aspects of God's delivering action Jonah prays. He prays when he is in the sea (2:4, 7), and he prays when he is in the belly of the fish (2:1). However inadequate these prayers may have been (there is, for example, no sign of Jonah's repentance), God freely responds with deliverance.

The psalm (verses 2-9) belongs to a type called the Song of Thanksgiving.[1] It is of the same order of psalm found elsewhere in the Old Testament (cf. Psalms 30, 32, 34, 107, 116). Generally speaking, these are psalms which express thanks to God for deliverance from the kinds of situations described in the laments (see, e.g., Psalms 7, 13). This is the song that is commonly referred to at the end of these laments (see Psalm 7:17, 13:6). The person in distress anticipates God's deliverance and the song he will sing in response.

Normally the song is sung in the presence of and even with the congregation (cf. Psalm 26:12, 40:9-10). It was accompanied by thank offerings. These actions were considered to be the payment of vows made while in distress (see Psalm 66:13-15, 116:17-19). However in Jonah (as, e.g., in Psalm 116) the payment of vows is necessarily delayed until a later time (verse 9).

There is a structure common to these Songs of Thanksgiving. Comparison with other Songs in the Psalter will assist in understanding this one.

1. Introduction. While varied, consists of an opening statement of praise, or reference to answered prayer or summary statement (verse 2). See also Psalm 30:1-2, 116:1-2.

2. Recollection of the distressful situation from which the person has been delivered, often with a quotation from the cry for help (verses 3-6a). Elements from the cry for help are found in verse 4. See Psalm 32:3-5, 116:3-4.

3. Report of the deliverance (verse 6b). See Psalm 116:5-11.

4. Conclusion (verses 7-9). This varies considerably in the different psalms. See Psalm 30:11-12, 32:6-11. Here it consists of a

recapitulation of the previous three elements in verse 7 (see below), the drawing of a lesson (verse 8), a vow (verse 9a) and a final statement of praise (verse 9b). But whatever the conclusion it is always the praise of God which is its goal.

The psalm of Jonah is thus quite typical. It was the type of psalm which the readers of the book would have sung on regular occasions. They, too, would have expressed their thankfulness to God upon deliverance from some distress. They can thus identify with Jonah here. And it should have been brought home to them how God has delivered them from troubles again and again even though they have deserved nothing of the sort. But even more, they should see in this song *the* appropriate response to *all* of God's acts of deliverance, not just Israel's.

One should observe that the progression of thought in verses 2-7 has a special character. Verse 2 states the pattern of distress, prayer to God for deliverance and answer to prayer. Verse 7 recapitulates this pattern. The intervening verses play on this pattern in an interesting way. Distress (verse 3) is followed by the prayer (verse 4), is followed again by distress (verses 5-6a) and then concludes with the answer to prayer (verse 6b).

The Fish

Numerous attempts have been made to identify the fish. None has met with any success. There are fish which could accommodate a person in their gullet. But inasmuch as the author uses the simple word for fish, it is unlikely that he has any particular kind of fish in mind.

There were a number of stories current in the ancient world about individuals (and even the entire crew of a ship!) surviving for a time in a fish. Thus this would probably not have been considered a unique phenomenon on the part of the author or his readers. Yet the author certainly intends the matter to be extraordinary and knew that it would capture the attention of his readers (see above, Chapter IV).

While the extraordinary is of interest here, the humorous is also. Humor is another way for the author to highlight the incongruity of Jonah's situation. He is transported back to land inside a fish's gut, mixed up with all sorts of other fish food! And then he was vomited up on the beach (and the Hebrew word says exactly that, not gently disembarked as some pictures would have it). It is as if to say that the fish can't put up with this character Jonah. He is relieved of his stomach troubles only when he gets rid of Jonah. Three days of undigested Jonah! And how silly Jonah must have felt being vomited head over heels across the sand dunes. It is enough to take the ego out of any man. Everything in all creation seems to be in a conspiracy with God to bring Jonah back to his senses.[2]

Aldous Huxley in his poem, "Jonah," has some lines that are striking here: "Seated on the convex mound of one vast kidney, Jonah prays and sings his canticles and hymns, making the hollow vault resound God's goodness and mysterious ways, till the great fish spouts music as he swims." That may well capture one aspect of this chapter: God's receiving praise in the most incongruous of places, the gut of a great fish swimming in the heart of the sea.

As for the primary significance of the fish, it should not be understood as the cause of the distress Jonah voices in the psalm. Notice that most of the psalm prayed in the belly of the fish (verse 1) is concerned with Jonah's experience *prior to* being swallowed by the fish (verses 2-6a). These verses recall his cry for help (with excerpts given in verse 4), as well as his near-drowning while at the mercy of the waves and currents of the sea. Verse 6b then makes clear that his life was saved from the depths of the sea. Thus, given the fact that the Song of *Thanksgiving* is prayed from the belly of the fish, it is the fish which must be understood as the vehicle for Jonah's deliverance from the sea. Jonah is saved by a fish! (On animals as a divine vehicle for deliverance, see 1 Kings 17:6.)

And yet Jonah's deliverance is not complete. He cannot survive for the rest of his days in the belly of the fish! And so God *finally* delivers Jonah by speaking to the fish and delivering Jonah onto dry land.[3]

Thus while the fish is not the vehicle of Jonah's final deliverance, it is clear that it is *not* a vehicle for God's judgment upon him. While most people might think being swallowed by a fish a horrifying experience, the author uses it as a preliminary vehicle for deliverance. The fish thus becomes another in the series of highly incongruous events in the book through which the author speaks (see Chapter IV). As we shall see, the fish also serves as a vehicle for returning Jonah to the place where he can be called to take up the task he had previously abandoned.

Three Days and Three Nights

It is not possible to say with any precision what the meaning of this phrase is.[4] The exact expression occurs elsewhere in the Old Testament only in 1 Samuel 30:12. The simple terms "three days" and "three nights" are quite common, however. They appear not to have reference to an exact period of time, only an approximation. (See, for example, the inexact usage of the phrase in Matthew 12:40. Jesus, of course, was not in the grave for three nights.)

While it is clear that this represents a significant period of deprivation for Jonah to be in a fish's belly and from which he would need to be delivered, there seems to be another interest here. Quite a few of the texts where the above phrases occur use them to refer to the period of a journey (see Genesis 22:4; Exodus 3:18; Numbers 33:8; Joshua 2:16). It is especially important to note the usage in Jonah 3:3. The same usage has been located in an extra-biblical text (the Sumerian "The Descent of Inanna into the Nether World"). But there the significance of the time period is even more specific, for it refers to the time it takes to travel from the earth to the underworld. This is especially striking because Jonah's journey goes from the underworld (2:2) back to earth (2:10).

It is possible then that the phrase "three days and three nights" refers to the amount of time it took for the fish to bring Jonah from Sheol back to earth. Thus the fish served as a "salt-water taxi." This would serve to stress the miraculous deliverance, for it specifies a journey or process from death to life.

This is not to suggest that the author of Jonah was familiar with the extra-biblical text. It simply means that there probably was a common understanding of this phrase current at the time of the author (and in Jesus' time?) which he makes use of in his book. (This might also serve as one more argument for the integrity of the psalm, for it is in the psalm that Jonah's being in Sheol is made explicit.)

It is important to be reminded that we are *not* dealing with the theme of resurrection in this chapter, at least as far as that term is normally used. Resurrection means not simply being raised *from* the dead, but raised *to* eternal life. Thus, e.g., Jesus' raising of Lazarus and the son of the widow of Nain are spoken of as resuscitations rather than resurrections, for both later died. Thus though it is clear that Jonah was more dead than alive when he was saved by the fish (see below), it is appropriate to speak only of his being resuscitated. (The parallel in Matthew 12:40 between Jesus and Jonah is concerned only with the three days and nights theme. Matthew does not say that Jesus will be resurrected like Jonah was. The New Testament witness is clear that Jesus was the first to be resurrected. See 1 Corinthians 15:20, 23.)

Life and Death

Life and death are important themes in the book (see above, Chapter III) and are especially prominent in the psalm. Before taking a brief look at this it is necessary to ask a preliminary question. Is the sea/water/death language of the psalm to be interpreted literally or figuratively (metaphorically)?

This difficulty is occasioned by the fact that in the psalms where this sort of language is often used, it is normally used figuratively to characterize deep distress. The sea/waters stood for all that was turbulent or chaotic, making for death in life, rather than referring to drowning. Thus Psalm 42:7, "All your waves and billows passed over me" (the exact language of Jonah 2:4), or Psalm 69:1, "Save me, O God, for the waters have come up to my neck. . . . I have come into deep waters, and the flood sweeps over me" (see Job 22:11; Isaiah 8:7-8).

As for Sheol, the abode of the dead, it is commonly used to refer to someone who has been delivered from near death, and hence not a literal reference to a trip to Sheol and back. Thus Psalm 30:3 (cf. Psalm 88:3-5; Ezekiel 28:8), "O Lord, thou hast brought up my soul from Sheol, restored me to life from among those gone down to the pit" (see Jonah 2:6).

It appears probable that the sea/water language in the book is to be understood *both* literally and figuratively (see Psalm 107:23-32; Exodus 15:5-10 for use of this language in a similar double way). The author appears to draw on a common fund of language (as used in the psalms noted above) to speak of that which the language literally describes. The amount of material dealing with the sea in the psalm is almost double that found in any other psalm. It appears to have been chosen because of its appropriateness to the context.

Yet the language used goes beyond the literal sense. For the reader familiar with all the metaphors in the psalms the language would have served to heighten the distress of Jonah. It would have had a kind of doubling effect on the reader.

This is true also for the language about Sheol. Inasmuch as Sheol was believed to be under the floor of the ocean (see Job 26:5), Jonah was spatially near the place. It is commonly stated that one "goes down" to Sheol (see Job 33:24; Psalm 22:29; Ezekiel 32:27-30). But Jonah was also at the point where he was more dead than alive (see 2:6). Jonah's flight is a descent into death (for "go down," see above, Chapter III).

Thus the language about Sheol is both literal and figurative. Again, the effect of this use of language would be to heighten the impact on the reader.

A few remarks about death and life are in order here.[5] In the Old Testament generally death is never understood simply in medical terms as the cessation of the brain wave or the heart beat. Any form of weakness or misery suffered in life is considered to be the intrusion of death into the sphere of life. Thus, e.g., to get sick is to experience death within life (see Isaiah 38:16; 2 Kings 5:7). Death is thus understood to be more a process than an event. It is a deterioration or, to use the imagery of the psalm, a "sinking." The greater the distress in which a person finds himself the more the reality of death that person experiences. This, of course, is not simply some reference to spiritual death, but to the death of the entire person.

On the other hand, life for the Hebrew is more than simply the presence of a heart beat. It must be characterized by a fullness, by all that makes for total well-being in all aspects of life, in order to be called life in any true sense (see Deuteronomy 30:19-20; Proverbs 19:23). But anything that brings new vitality (that contributes to such well-being) can be described as life-giving. Even a cup of cold water (see Judges 15:19) or a piece of good news (see Genesis 45:27).

As for Jonah's place in that death process, life (in every respect!) has ebbed so much that he could be reckoned more among the dead than among the living. "I went down to the land (i.e., Sheol) whose bars closed upon me forever" (2:6). We have similar idioms in modern speech, though they tend to be used much too easily (e.g., "I'm dead" or "I've been through hell").

It is striking the degree to which Jonah's experience of death in Chapter 2 is parallel to his experience in Chapter 4. There, too, life has become distressful for him and death so pervasive. Ironically, it is the giving of life to Nineveh that results in the deterioration of life in Jonah.

The Song of Thanksgiving

We must now take a brief look at some of the individual verses of the psalm. In 2:2 Jonah refers to his prayer for deliverance before he was rescued by the fish. Verse 4 contains a portion of the prayer that he prayed at that time. Verse 7 also refers to this when it states that he remembered the Lord, meaning, he turned to God in prayer. Verse 2 summarizes much of the psalm with its reference to the distress, the prayer and the deliverance (cf. Psalm 30:2-3, 18:6, 120:1). In spite of all that Jonah had done, God listened and answered his prayer.

Jonah recalls that he cried to the Lord out of "Sheol" (the words "land" and "Pit" in verse 6 also refer to Sheol). We have indicated above that it is to be understood in both a literal and a figurative way. Sheol was the place of the dead. It was considered a place lacking in possessions (Psalm 49:17f.), memory (Psalm 88:11, 13), knowledge (Ecclesiastes 9:10), possibility of return (Job 7:9f., 10:22, 16:22), and end (Jeremiah 51:39; Job 14:12), but also lacking in torture and annihilation. Its inhabitants were called "shades" (see Job 26:5), comparable to our "only a shadow of his former self," only much stronger. Most distressing of all, however, is that it was considered a place largely cut off from God (see Psalm 88:5, 10-12, 115:17; Isaiah 38:18), beyond his presence, though not beyond his power (see Amos 9:2; Prov. 15:11; Ps. 139:8). The repeated use of this language shows the depths of Jonah's distress and how death was more characteristic of him than life.

In verse 3 Jonah begins to expand upon his distress (cf. Psalm 42:7). It is striking that he ascribes his brush with drowning not simply to the consequences of his own rebellion, but as a consequence of God's actions (see 1:12). He realizes that it was finally God who had caused him to be thrown into the sea, and that it is God's waves and billows which are swirling around him. Jonah sees that the pagan sailors were just agents of God in carrying out his will. Again, the sea language must be understood both figuratively and literally (as also in verses 5-6). Literally, the "flood" has reference to sea currents (see Psalm 18:4) and the "heart of the seas" to their most remote areas (see Micah 7:19).

Verse 4 is a little perplexing, not least because of the way in which it is commonly translated (the Hebrew text does not need to be emended as in the RSV, and should be translated, "I am cast out [or, driven away] from thy presence, *nevertheless* I shall again look upon thy holy temple."). The clue to its understanding is verse 7, where it is stated that Jonah's prayer did come to God's temple (i.e., God's dwelling place, heaven, or its earthly symbol in Jerusalem, cf. Psalm 18:6, 11:4). The psalmist is thus not wondering whether he will ever see the temple again. Rather, the verse simply indicates that he is looking to God in prayer. He is going to pray even though he wonders whether his prayer will be heard. He has been driven far from God's presence, i.e., God is so far because death is so near (see Psalm 88:5), and he asks whether communication with him is still possible (see Psalm 31:22).

Verses 5-6 return to the theme of Jonah's distress in the sea (see Psalm 18:4, 69:1, 116:3). He gets all tangled up in sea vegetation (this shows clearly that he is in the sea and not in the belly of the fish) and finds himself at the bottom of the ocean where it was believed the bases of the mountains were located (see Deuteronomy 32:22). He is now beyond the point of rescuing himself. The bars (gates) of Sheol have closed in upon him. Left to his own power, death is now inevitable. The death process has gotten to the point where he is helplessly in its grip; no self-reversal is possible. Only *God* can bring him back to life. And he does (verse 6b, see Psalm 30:3)! His confessional response is "O Lord my God."

Verse 7 returns once again to the situation of distress and recapitulates the entire psalm to this point. "My soul fainted within me." The word "soul" here means simply life and hence indicates that his life was at a very low ebb, indeed was at the point of being extinguished (see Psalm 107:5). Again the point is that he was more dead than alive. In the midst of this distress he remembers God, that is, he meditates or turns to God in prayer (see Psalm 63:6, 77:3, 6). He now knows that his prayer did come before God because he has been delivered (see Psalm 18:6).

Verse 8 is a difficult verse, not least because of the rather sudden change in mood. He now proceeds to contrast all idol-worshipers with his own behavior toward God (see Psalm 31:6). This would appear to be highly ironical (see above, Chapter IV). He suggests that he is different from those who rely on idols when they get into trouble. He relies only upon the Lord. What he forgets is that he himself has fled (forsaken) God ("true loyalty," see Psalm 144:2, RSV note) for the idolatry of a particular belief. Jonah by seeking to limit God has made God over into his own image, and thus he has fallen into the same idolatry of which he here accuses others. In the absence of any repentance on Jonah's part, it would appear as if he here seeks to cover up his own disloyalty with language that sets him apart from others who do not praise God as he does.

In verse 9 Jonah vows to bring a thank-offering when he returns home. He does exactly what the heathen have done (1:16). Their responses are identical. He then concludes his Song with a statement of praise. "Deliverance belongs to the Lord!"

This line is striking in terms of the larger context of the book. When Jonah is delivered (both here and in 4:6) he reacts to *his own* deliverance with thanks and praise. This stands in sharp contrast to his reaction to the deliverance of Nineveh. God's deliverance extended to Jonah in spite of his *lack* of repentance would be denied by Jonah to those who have in fact repented. It would appear that deliverance is something Jonah *expects* from God. As such, his confession, "Deliverance belongs to the Lord!" stands in brilliant incongruity to the limitation which Jonah places on that very deliverance when it comes to the Ninevites. For Jonah, in the final analysis, God should *not* be able to extend his deliverance to whomever he pleases.

This line may well serve as the key verse of the book. It is true for the sailors in Chapter 1, for Jonah in Chapter 2, for the Nine-vites in Chapter 3, and it is the objective of God's questioning of Jonah in Chapter 4. The idea of deliverance, of God's *not* extend-ing to people what they deserve, is at the very center of the argument between God and Jonah. For Jonah, God's actions must be appropriately related to human conduct. Judgment must fall upon the wicked. God, however, is free to break into the continuum of sin and punishment and deliver. His ways cannot be limited by what is customary in human behavior. Deliverance belongs to the Lord. It cannot be circumscribed by Jonah or any-one else. Israel has needed such a God in the past and, just as much as the Ninevites, stands in need of such a God again and again.

It would thus appear as if the psalm does not reveal any de-cisive change in Jonah. He has not repented to God at all. The juxtaposition of a conflict of beliefs with a continuing life of faith seems to continue here. Yet, does not his going to Nineveh in the next chapter reveal some basic change in him? To that we must now turn.

Notes

1. J. Eaton, *The Psalms*, SCM, 1965.

2. Good, pp. 46-47.

3. J. Watts, *The Books of Joel, Obadiah, Jonah, Nahum, Habakkuk and Zephaniah*, p. 87.

4. Landes, p. 11.

5. On the "womb of Sheol" and other conceptions of death and the underworld so prevalent in this chapter, see N. Tromp, *Primitive Conceptions of Death and the Nether World in the Old Testa-ment*, Rome, 1969.

VIII

FROM

KING

TO BARNYARD

Jonah 3:1-10

We want to begin this chapter with a few observations regarding structure (see above, Chapter IV). It is to be noted that the first verses of this chapter are almost identical to those of Chapter 1. Jonah is given essentially the same command by an incredibly patient God: "Arise, go and call . . ." This technique is devised to create suspense in the minds of the readers. What will Jonah do this time? This time Jonah arises . . . and goes to Nineveh "according to the word of the Lord." (Why he goes this time will be considered later in this chapter.) The two chapters are also developed in a similar manner. After the response from the group as a whole, the leader (captain, king) emerges, and efforts are made to avert disaster. Both chapters end in deliverance.

Verses 4-10 follow a threefold pattern relatively common among Old Testament materials: (a) threatened disaster (verse 4), (b) acts of penitence (verses 5-9), (c) deliverance (verse 10). See the parallels in Joel 2:11-19; 1 Samuel 7:3-11; Jeremiah 18:7-11; Ezra 8:21-23; Esther 4. Except for the passage in Jeremiah these parallels have to do only with Israel.

In Jeremiah 18 reference is made to the fact that this threefold pattern is applicable not only to Israel but to all peoples: "If at any time I declare concerning a nation or a kingdom, that I will pluck up and break down and destroy it, and if that nation, concerning which I have spoken, turns from its evil, I will repent of the evil that I intended to do to it." Jonah 3 might be considered an illustration of what Jeremiah states in more abstract form. The point of the parallel structure seems to be: Israel and Nineveh are dealt with in the *same* way by God. God has no favorites. No special treatment can be expected by Israel from God and God is not being more lenient with people like the Ninevites than he has been with Israel. But even more, the heathen here become models for Israel!

In this regard the Joel 2 passage is a particularly instructive parallel to Jonah 3.[1] It is possible that the two works are nearly contemporaneous, which would make the point even more striking. It shows that Israel, like Nineveh, must also walk the road of repentance. It also indicates that God's merciful deliverance is for Israel too a gracious act, an act that moves well beyond what the people actually deserve. Joel is concerned with a threatened Jerusalem (2:1-11). The call goes out for repentance and acts of penitence (2:12-17). Everyone, from great to small, is expected to participate (2:16, cf. Jonah 3:5). Upon Israel's response God repents regarding the judgment (2:18-19).

God is seen as repenting regarding Israel's destruction in a manner quite apart from the question of justice. If one were to ask into Israel's *just* desserts, then God should *not* have had pity. But God's saving action moves beyond justice. If the author of Jonah knew Joel, the point made would be very clear: If this has been the case with Israel in the past, then Israel has no right to raise the question of justice regarding God's deliverance of Nineveh. Israel and Nineveh are parallel people in the eyes of God. God's grace works in the same way for everyone.

The author's purposive use of exaggeration is especially prominent in this chapter (see Chapter IV above). The size of the city of Nineveh (3:3) is described in terms much larger than was actually the case. This huge city, great in size and population, experiences a total conversion, extending even to the animals! What more striking way could be found to emphasize the potential effect that the preaching of the Word of God could have on even (for Israel) the worst examples of humankind. Moreover, it was only *one* man preaching to an empire! How unreasonable, even absurd, to think that the work of one person could have such an effect. At the same time, this serves to stress the burden of responsibility which lies upon those who have been given the Word to speak.

Jonah's Halfhearted Efforts

So that the point becomes even clearer we should have an overview of what Jonah does in Nineveh according to verses 3-4. First of all, it is to be noted that Jonah only "begins to go" into the city, going only one day's journey. We have no reason to infer that he went any farther. Thus, much of the city never heard of him at all. While this may suggest that he makes little effort to get the task done well, it also makes doubly striking the fact that the entire city responds nevertheless. One has to think of a massive chain reaction, of neighbor telling neighbor until the news reaches all (see verse 6, "and the tidings reached the king").

So much of the response to Jonah's message is thus indirect. Yet what an effect! The Ninevites themselves become involved in the spreading of the Word. Everything and everyone seems to be conspiring to see that Jonah *succeeds!*

Second, Jonah is said to have spoken only a poorly communicated message. Only five words (in Hebrew) are given us. While it is not clear that this is all he had to say, it suggests that his message was rather brief and that it was quite repetitive. Moreover, there is no reason to believe that it was spoken in a language other than Hebrew. And this in a city where only a few, if any, would have known the language (though some would have known a closely related language). And yet, in spite of all this lack of good communication skills, the city responds in overwhelming fashion.

Third, Jonah's message was a rather truncated one. There is no reason to think that anything else he had to say was of a different sort from that reported in verse 4. It was entirely a message of doom, with no reasons given (the same language is used of the destruction of Sodom and Gomorrah in Genesis 19:25, 29). Jonah's message was thus incomplete when compared to other messages of the prophets against foreign nations. Thus, for example, there is no mention at all of the sins the people have committed (see Amos 1-2).

Moreover, to specify a brief time limit such as forty days was unexampled among the prophets. The closest are Isaiah 7:8 and Jeremiah 25:11-12, which refer to rather extensive periods of time, and are *not* spoken to the people involved. It would thus appear as if Jonah did *not* proclaim exactly "the message that I tell you" (3:2).

Jonah thus makes his message as vague and as blunt and as offensive as he possibly can. It is suggested that he delivered a message that would make it almost impossible for the people to respond positively. And yet they do so in a manner quite beyond the realm of human calculation. Jonah thus went to Nineveh obediently, but the conflict with God had not yet been resolved (see above, Chapter I). As a result his message was affected.

Moreover, it might be noted that this message was delivered by a man who had just been saved by God from death in the sea. Jonah had just experienced the unmerited grace and goodness of God in his own life. Now he turns right around and makes it as difficult as possible for the Ninevites to experience God's deliverance. No mention of sins to which they might repent, no glimmer of hope, just forty days and wham! A graceless message delivered by one living in the shadow of an experience of grace.

And yet no preacher has ever met with such success. Little

effort, poor skills, a terrible sermon—and total success. And a *foreign* prophet, quite unknown to the Ninevites! God had prepared a way for this message so that in spite of the missionary it found its way into the hearts of the Ninevites. God *can* write straight with crooked lines. God can use even false prophets to accomplish his purposes. With such intractable human material God has worked, and continues to work. The place of the messenger is crucial in God's ways of working with the world, but so often it seems as if the messenger hinders more than helps.

We are now better enabled to return to a question left unanswered at the beginning of this chapter: Why did Jonah obey God's command this time around? From all appearances he goes without a word of protest or a murmur of complaint. Yet there is no indication whatsoever that Jonah has had any change of heart in the conflict between himself and God. That he goes "according to the word of the Lord" (3:3) means nothing other than that he now obeys the command (see above, Chapter I). There is no indication that the experience with the sea and the fish have chastened him, or that he has repented of his former actions, or that he now resolves to change his theological tune. There is no evidence that Jonah now goes to Nineveh in gratitude to God for his own deliverance.

We have seen in the previous paragraphs, however, some evidence for the fact that Jonah goes to Nineveh with some reluctance. It would appear to be a half-hearted move on his part, dragging his feet all the way. And then carrying out the task in such a way as if to be assured that the Ninevites would *not* respond positively to his message. It is almost as if he says to himself: "How can I do this so that there is the least possible chance for the Ninevites to repent and be delivered from destruction?"

Chapter 4:2 also makes it very clear that he still thinks the reasons he had for not going to Nineveh in the first place are valid. In getting angry at the results of his preaching, he clearly reveals that his motives in preaching in the first place were not what they should have been. He doesn't want to admit that God's approach to the wicked Ninevites may be right. The question as to his motive for going to Nineveh thus still remains.

One factor seems to be a realization that he cannot escape from God. God has pursued him across the sea and down to the very gates of Sheol. He realizes now that he cannot avoid the task. He has no option but to resign himself to his fate. And so he goes, yet determined to do the job in such a way that the results that God wants (i.e., the repentance of the Ninevites) will not be forthcoming.

Another factor may well be Jonah's recognition that, if Nineveh did not respond, they might be destroyed even sooner than would otherwise be the case. And so to effect this he attaches the unparalleled forty-day limit for response to his message. Jonah not only makes his message difficult to respond to, but also gives them a minimum of time in which to do it. (One might also note that he thereby seeks to force God to act according to a predetermined timetable. Jonah is forever wanting God to do things his way!) Jonah knows God's merciful inclinations, but he also knows that, if faith and repentance are not forthcoming (and he'll help that along all he can!) destruction will occur. And so Jonah goes, under some duress and without mercy in his heart, hoping that he can effect the judgment that the wicked Ninevites deserve. And if he can do that, all of his troubles will have been worthwhile.

Nineveh's Wholehearted Response

We have seen how Jonah, though trying to be unsuccessful, succeeds in converting the wicked metropolis. The details the author uses in depicting this in verses 4-9 are deliberately overdrawn in order to highlight the irony of the prophet's totally unexpected success. The author, of course, intends the result to surprise everyone.

The entire city, from the least of them to the greatest (3:5), responds positively to the message. The king himself comes down from his throne, removes all signs of his royal authority, and now obligates all citizens to engage in acts of penitence. Inasmuch as the people had already fully responded (3:5), the decree of the king amounts to a royal seal of approval on what had occurred spontaneously. It becomes, as it were, government policy. Inasmuch as the king in that part of the ancient Near East was considered to be semi-divine, it might be said that in the king's action even divine authority bows before the God of Jonah. Everyone from god to beast!

Even the animals are involved. (The word "beast" covers the animal world in contrast to human beings, while "herd and flock" further specify this as having reference to all large and small domesticated animals.) They are required to do everything that the people are: put on sackcloth, neither feed nor drink, cry to God and turn from their ways of violence. Beasts are commonly specified as participants in God's judgment (see Jeremiah 21:6). Involvement of animals in rites of mourning was not unknown in the ancient world either (see Judith 4:10, Herodotus), but never to this extent. The author intends thereby to stress the prophet's success. St. Francis preached to the animals, but only Jonah in the history of preaching ever brought about the prayer and repentance of sheep and goats! He may also have intended to contrast Nineveh's response to Israel's at this point. The animals are more responsive to God than Israel (see Isaiah 1:3).

One other item descriptive of the response to Jonah is deserving of attention: "And they believed God" (3:5). As in Genesis 15:6 and Exodus 14:31, it is not simply a matter of believing that Jonah's prediction would come true. They responded in true faith to God.

It is noteworthy that they believed God even though there is no mention of God at all in Jonah's message of 3:4. Comparison with the sailors' response in chapter 1 is instructive here. The sailors respond to the Lord (Yahweh) in verses 14, 16. The Ninevites respond only to "God" (verses 5, 8, 9).

While this interpretation is uncertain, the difference in the response may be related to the different statements of Jonah in 1:9 and 3:4. Only in the former is the covenant name of the God of Israel revealed. In 3:4 no name is given at all. The Ninevites simply infer that "God" (the general name for deity in that part of the world) is involved. This difference may well serve to stress the importance of the human messenger in articulating the Word of God. The nature of the human response to God is in large part determined by the way in which the message is articulated. Not the least of the tasks of the messenger is the naming of the name of God.

It is also striking here that the heathen *do* draw the conclusion that God is involved. They could have drawn a variety of conclusions. It was not necessary to infer that God was now involved in their lives. To Israelites thinking that God was no longer active in their affairs, who think that God has forgotten them, this response of the Ninevites would seem to be a model of how they ought to be more ready to recognize his action in the inarticulate events that occur around them.

The Repentance of God

One comment made by the king of Nineveh is especially striking (3:9): "Who knows, God may yet repent and turn from his fierce anger, so that we perish not." This motif occurs also in 1:6 and 1:14.

Who knows? This statement by the captain reflects a very sophisticated understanding of God and his activity in the world.[2] It is relatively common elsewhere in the Old Testament (see Exodus 32:30; Amos 5:15; Zephaniah 2:3; Lamentations 3:29; Joel 2:14). That this understanding should be found only on the lips of the heathen (captain, sailors, king) is one of the ironic features of the book. It is the heathen rather than Jonah who have such extraordinary insight into the sovereign freedom of God. They, in fact, articulate what Jonah refuses to allow in his

God: God acts as it pleases him, which may or may not conform to human expectations.

How are we to understand this "Who knows?", this "divine perhaps"? In the most fundamental sense it is a reference to the sovereign freedom of God's actions. Thus, while Nineveh's repentance was a necessary condition for God's repentance, it was not in and of itself sufficient. God's action rested finally on his own sovereign decision.

The heathen thus ironically understand clearly that their repentance is not something magical which would *automatically* result in God's grace being extended to them and judgment removed. While God's saving action is normally contingent upon some kind of human response, God does not *have* to act mercifully if humans so respond. There is no mechanical relationship between human acts of piety or worship and God's saving action. Repentance does not *entitle* one to salvation.

While God is indeed motivated to save because of human prayer and repentance, God remains ultimately free to decide for himself what he will do. For no human act, however repentant or pious or worthy of commendation, is finally sufficient to make God's saving action *necessary,* or the only possible action on his part.[3] His action is finally grounded totally in himself. And thus, if he chooses to deliver, this is an act of pure grace. That God's grace was active even prior to human repentance is evident in the mere fact that the Ninevites had a message from God to which to respond.

What is true of God's delivering actions is also true of his judgmental activity. These actions of God are parallel as they relate to God's sovereign freedom. Just as God's judgment is not an automatic consequence of sin (God may repent!), so God's pity is not a necessary consequence of repentance (perhaps!).

The use of the word "repentance" for God in this context can be confusing (3:9, 10, 4:2). This word is normally used in connection with human repentance or turning away from sin. Here, however, repentance refers to God's decision to turn away from a decision previously made because of a change in circumstances (i.e., the repentance of the people). In this chapter, God thus decides that, in the light of the people's repentance, he will save them rather than follow through on his previous decision to destroy them because of their wickedness. This is what the king of Nineveh hoped for.

The Old Testament is not at all embarrassed about saying that God changes his plan (see Exodus 32:12, 14; Amos 7:3, 6; Jeremiah 18:7-11, 26:2-3). Again and again the Old Testament witnesses to the fact that God is responsive to his creatures. He does not set his mind on some matter relating to his people and then pursue it to its conclusion irrespective of how they may respond. As people change, as history develops, God will be responsive to what is happening and adjust his ways and means.

And yet always in view will be God's ultimate salvific will for his creatures. *That* will remain unchangeable! But it is precisely in the light of that unchangeable will of God for the salvation of his world (see Ezekiel 18:23, 32) that he *will* change his course of action in the light of human response.

This makes it quite clear that God is not capricious in his actions, so that the community of faith is left in a perpetual state of anxiety regarding the course of his action. The confession of 4:2 makes it evident that God's will is to save his people. His steadfast love and his wrath are not equally primary attributes. God will *always* act in ways that are consonant with his ultimate goal of salvation for his world. But such a confession of faith is not reducible to a formula whereby it can be determined just how God will act in *specific* cases. The "divine perhaps" thus safeguards the divine sovereignty and enables grace to remain truly grace.

The Ninevites are thus thankful for a God who is willing and able to change. Only with such a God would it be possible finally for anyone to live. Without that the destructive fate of all the Ninevites (and the Jonahs!) of the world would have been settled long ago. They are able to live by the fact that God, who abounds in steadfast love, can change and turn aside the end truly deserved by all. But no one is able to get beyond the point of asking the question of the king of Nineveh: Who knows?

And so God in his response to Nineveh does not follow through on his announced judgment upon the city. "And God saw what they did." This should be understood, not simply in terms of their acts of fasting, but in terms of their entire response to God. There is an integral relationship between human "turning" and divine "turning" (see above, Chapter III). It is clear that the human response to God is crucial. Yet the context also makes it clear that finally God's response of deliverance is grounded in his love.

Two points of contrast between Jonah (Israel) and Nineveh are certainly intended in this chapter. Jonah, a member of the people God has chosen to be his own, remains unresponsive in the face of a long history of divine activity. On the other hand, the heathen respond at the first word from God that they hear. More particularly, Jonah remains unmoved by his sins against God, while the Ninevites are open to repentance.

The author certainly hoped that it would begin to dawn upon his readers that "the wicked Ninevites" are not some special case in God's world that proves that God is unjust. Rather, they should begin to see that, in the final analysis, the Ninevites are no worse in the sight of God than Israel is. On behalf of both peoples God has acted again and again in a way that goes beyond justice.

There is also a theological contrast between the two peoples. Jonah prefers a God who does not repent indiscriminately. And that now becomes the subject of the first verses of Chapter 4.

Notes

1. Cf. Wolff, pp. 69-70.
2. See J. Jeremias, *Die Reue Gottes,* Neukirchen, 1975, pp. 98-109; K. Miskotte, *When the Gods Are Silent,* pp. 432-3; Wolff, p. 113.
3. Landes, p. 128.

IX

DO YOU

BEGRUDGE

MY GENEROSITY?

Jonah 4:1-11

We must first of all take a look at whatever structures may be present in this chapter. It appears as if it is ordered in a way similar to Chapter 1, an ABCCBA chiasmus:

A. Report/Question (4:1-2)
  1. Jonah's anger (1).
  2. Jonah's question (2).

B. Request/Question (4:3-4)

  1. Jonah requests death (3).
  2. God questions Jonah (4).

C. Jonah's Response/God's Response (4:5-6a)
  1. Jonah builds hut (5).
  2. God gives plant to save Jonah (6a).

A¹. Report/Question (4:9b-11)
  1. Jonah's anger (9b).
  2. God's question (10-11).

B¹. Request/Question (4:8b-9a)
  1. Jonah requests death (8b).
  2. God questions Jonah (9a).

C¹. Jonah's Response/God's Response (4:6b-8a)
  1. Jonah very glad (6b).
  2. God kills plant to afflict Jonah (7-8a).

The full impact of this structure will become evident as we proceed. Two brief notes may be in order here. First of all, note the reports of Jonah's anger and requests for death. These are very strong statements. In the first instance, Jonah was *exceedingly* angry because of Nineveh's deliverance. In the second instance, he was angry enough to die because of the destruction of his plant. In each case his anger is directed at God's actions. Even more, it is directed at the full range of God's actions, from deliverance to destruction. It is striking that midway between these two expressions of anger Jonah expresses "great joy" (verse 6). This occurs when *he* experiences deliverance. This is parallel to verse 5 where Jonah sits tight to his conviction that Nineveh should be *destroyed*. Thus fundamental to the conflict between Jonah and God is the question of the *object* of God's actions of deliverance and destruction.

Second, note the parallel questions in verses 2, 10-11. Jonah's question reaffirms his conviction that God's mercy results in unjust actions toward those who deserve the consequences of their wickedness. God's question to Jonah points out that, if Jonah claims the right to feel sorrow over a plant which is not even his, surely God has a right to be merciful toward his own creation without being subject to the charge of injustice.

Jonah Angry Because God Is Not

We now turn to the text.[1] Jonah's reaction in 4:1 is psychologically almost incomprehensible (see above, Chapter III for anger motif). That a prophet who has been called will not preach is strange. Stranger still is that Jonah becomes angry at the deliverance of the Ninevites and reproaches God for his gracious actions. "Really now, God!" And this shocking reaction is compounded when it is seen that Jonah himself is alive only because of this very same grace active on his behalf. He himself had just been so graciously delivered from the depths of the sea, from death itself, and quite undeservedly at that. And now he wants to place a limitation on that very same grace. It is all right apparently for God to be gracious to *him*, but to extend the same benefits to the evil Ninevites is quite another question.

I suppose that if anything is sin, this is. Rebellion against grace. Resistance to God's gracious activity on behalf of others, however evil they may be. I did not bear witness, I did not want to go, because I was afraid, God, that you who are abundant in steadfast love would repent of the promised judgment and save Nineveh rather than pour out your wrath in destruction (4:2).

It is thus made clear in 4:2 that the issue at stake between God and Jonah lies at the very heart of Israel's understanding of her faith: "Thou art a gracious God and merciful, slow to anger, and abounding in steadfast love and repentest of evil." This statement has virtually the status of a creed in ancient Israel. It occurs some ten times (Exodus 34:6-7; Joel 2:13; Numbers 14:18; Nehemiah 9:17; Psalm 86:15; 103:8; 145:8; Nahum 1:3; 2 Chronicles 30:9) and is alluded to in many other places (e.g., Psalm 111:4; 112:4; 116:8). Psalm 145:8-9 may be especially important here because the creed applies in this passage not simply to Israel, but to "all that he has made."

The essence of this confession is the affirmation of the *priority of grace* in all of God's dealings with his creatures. God's mercy and God's wrath are not equally important ways of speaking about God's relationship with his world. God's wrath issuing in judgment is clearly his "foreign" work. When judgment is seen to be necessary because of human sin, God hopes against hope that he will not have to carry through on what the people deserve (see Hosea 11:8-9). This understanding is intensified in the confession used in Jonah (and Joel) by the addition of the words, "and repents of evil." This phrase sharpens the idea that God is one who ever stands ready to change his decision of judgment and exercise mercy (see above, Chapter VIII).

Jonah does not disagree with this confession in and of itself. As we have seen, his problem is that God is indiscriminate in his exercise of his mercy. He is too much like an indulgent father who spares the rod and spoils the child. God is too lenient a judge. He stands too ready to forgive the guilty and let the punishment go unrendered. There comes a point when God must not let the evil go unpunished. This is certainly the case with the wicked Ninevites. And so Jonah believes that this confession is fundamentally a sound one, but God must use greater care in restricting its sphere of operation. Jonah does not seem to understand that his own history in the depths of the sea has revealed (again and again!) that he is alive because of the exercise of that same grace, though he deserved only punishment. God's grace is not the possession of the elect. It is not at their disposal to do with, to dispense, as they see fit. It is something which they, too, are continually *given* without any merit on their part.

As a consequence of what God has done on behalf of the Ninevites, Jonah asks God to take his life. Jonah asks God to kill him! This is an extraordinary response to the situation on his part. It is very difficult to understand how, just because a city has been saved from the judgment, Jonah doesn't want to live anymore. What kind of mental state must Jonah have been in that he should respond in such an extreme manner? Is this not a sign of mental instability on his part, a defect in his character? When one sees how rare indeed a death wish is in the Old Testament, it becomes even more striking.

I think that Jonah's response reveals that his problem with God is not simply at the intellectual level. Jonah is not simply on some kind of "head trip," some esoteric discussion that has little relationship to life as it actually has to be lived. The struggle between God and Jonah is fundamentally theological in character, but it is a theological conflict that lies very close to life.

The situation as sketched out in Chapter II needs to be recalled here. Israel has been subjected to severe hardships in life: subject to foreign powers, economic difficulties affecting daily life and health, a highly uncertain future. This is life in the Israelite community for whom the prophets had promised a glorious future. It was thus a community characterized in significant ways by disappointment and despair. And it is to this kind of community that the word to go to Nineveh comes. Life is now to be offered to the wicked, while Israel continues to suffer a life of distress. How can that be? What sense does that make? If God's actions are so contrary not only to previous promises but also to simple rules of fair play, then something terrible has gone wrong with the basic order of things. And now, when in fact such wicked people are delivered, and Israel is still ekeing out a living, life must have seemed horribly out of kilter. *Nineveh* is the recipient of God's promises. "Our faith in God must have been in vain. All of our lives wasted on this commitment!" Life must indeed have seemed futile (see above, Chapter II).

It is some such situation which we must presuppose if we are going to understand this heart-wrenching death wish on the part of Jonah.

One point of relationship to a motif we saw in Chapter VI may be in order here. There we noted how bad theology may lead to disobedience. Here we see how bad theology may also lead to despair. If the Israelites had not had such a limited understanding of their God, an understanding that, among other things, tied together much too closely faith in God and social/political/economic prosperity, they would have been better enabled to cope with the realities of life (see below, Chapter X).

Finally, in connection with this motif, we should note the interesting parallel between Jonah and Elijah. Listen to 1 Kings 19:4, "And Elijah asked that he might die, saying, 'It is enough. Now, O Lord, take away my life, for I am no better than my fathers.'" The difference between Jonah and Elijah is striking. Elijah was in despair over his *failure* to turn the hearts of the idolatrous people of Israel. Jonah was in despair over his *success*. Jonah's response is thus pictured as being precisely opposite that which it should be. He should have rejoiced over this event, just as he later was to rejoice over the plant that delivered him from the heat. But instead of joy there is anger, anger to the point of wishing to die.

One of the more important motifs in these opening verses is anger (see above, Chapter III). Jonah's anger at the results of his preaching (4:1, 4) are set over against God's slowness to anger (4:2). Jonah has become angry because God has refused to pour out his anger (cf. 3:9). Jonah will be angry if God will not be. He thus arrogates to himself a godlike reaction in this situation.

This point is made especially clear by God's question to Jonah (4:3), "Is it right for you to be angry?" That is, about the deliverance of the city. The essence of this question is: Are you right in passing judgment upon God's sovereign decision *not* to be angry? Jonah believes himself to be responding in proper fashion in this situation. This is, of course, nothing less than a judgment of God! More particularly, a judgment on God's right to be slow to anger. Jonah judges God's *salvation-act* to be worthy only of a wrathful response.

God's Patient Response

Verse 4 portrays a marvelous image of the tenderness of God in the face of Jonah's judgmental anger. God does not break off the conversation. He refuses to acquiesce when Jonah asks him to take his life. Even for such a one, God does not want death! Here the Lord of history, who rules the wind and the sea and the mighty denizens of the deep, who saves a wicked heathen metropolis, stoops to hold a conversation with a rebellious child. What patience! What unmotivated fairness!

But Jonah sees nothing of such fairness or patience. He hears only the judgment of God that his anger has not been an appropriate response. Hence he treats the question with utter silence. The scene portrayed in 4:5 illustrates that silence in a striking fashion (whether or not this verse is a delayed report from Chapter 3:4, it serves the author's purpose in this way).

Jonah responds, not by picking up his marbles and going

home, but by challenging God with the firmness of his resolve. He will hold to his convictions! God had better take another look at the situation and the city. 4:5 thus makes clear the unchanged mind-set of Jonah, a perspective firmly set on the destruction of the Ninevites as the only just outcome of their evil deeds.

An impasse between God and Jonah is evident, not unlike that which occasioned Jonah's flight in the first place. Something comparable to the wind on the sea is needed again. This time, however, God takes a different tack. Rather than sending something destructive, he sends something beneficial. Rather than a storm, Jonah gets a plant. Rather than being exposed to the elements, he gets protected from them.

God's purpose in sending the plant (4:6) was not simply directed toward protecting Jonah from the heat of the sun, however. He also had the intention of "saving him from his evil" (the translation, "discomfort," is possible, but unlikely in view of the previous clause which expresses this idea. The presence of the key word "evil" also suggests this interpretation, see above, Chapter III).

One wonders why Jonah needed a plant when he already had his little hut. The shelter he built for himself may have been rather insubstantial, but the plant is probably to be understood as an extra bonus provided by God for the occasion. Anyone who has sat in a tent for a day in the Near East understands that additional shade is always welcome!

Attempts to determine the kind of plant have not been altogether successful. The author may have been thinking of the castor oil plant. This plant had very large leaves, suitable for providing shade. Possibly one ought to understand it as an ad hoc plant, one provided by God especially for the occasion. In any case, it is a merciful action on God's part (the destruction of the plant is not yet in view, for the sequence of events is determined by Jonah's response to the new situation). In spite of Jonah's continuing anger at God and his attitude toward God's gracious activity, God provides relief for Jonah. God answers the complaint and the anger with a miracle of deliverance. One would now think that Jonah would suddenly realize how God's grace is extended even and always toward those who are undeserving of it.

And so there he sits in the shadow of God's generosity. How does he react?

Jonah reacts with "great joy." Period. What could explain this sudden transition from anger so severe as to wish for death to great joy? As is emphasized in Hebrew, he is not just happy; he is deliriously happy! Unless one wishes to ascribe such sharp highs and lows in Jonah's responses to mental instability, one needs to remember again the situation we have sketched out. God has now provided for his people in some miraculous fashion! Perhaps this is a sign that the great promises of the prophets are on their way to fulfillment.

The irony of Jonah's self-centered response is striking. Here is some small token which God has extended to Jonah concerning which he virtually leaps for joy. Yet when a much greater benefit is extended to the wicked Ninevites his reaction is "great anger" (note that the reactions in both verses 1 and 6 are described with the word "exceedingly"). As was the case when he was delivered from the sea, when God's deliverance extended to *him,* he is right in tune with the confession of God's steadfast love, but not when it is extended to people like the Ninevites.

Putting Jonah in a Corner

Given Jonah's reaction to the plant, God responds with some further "appointments." This time it is a worm, just at dawn, when the sun starts to warm things up. A worm appointed to turn a worm. It causes the plant to dry up (within minutes!).

Then a hot east wind is appointed. This is no doubt intended to refer to the sirocco, a dust-laden, furnacelike blast of heat that parches the body by evaporating perspiration. When this wind blows today in that part of the world, it is not unusual for the temperatures to reach 110 degrees and the humidity to get as low as 2 percent!

God's ways with Jonah are quite transparent here. Destruction now comes, not upon Nineveh, but upon something that had become very important to Jonah, something which had brought him great joy. He is thus given a little taste of what it is like to experience destruction. In his "fainting" (4:8) he again experiences death within life, as in 2:7. A kind of preliminary judgment is here passed on Jonah rather than upon Nineveh. God hopes that he will now be able to draw the obvious conclusion from this experience: If this is what it is like to experience God's judgment, I want no part of it for the Ninevites either.

Jonah's response, however, is not that at all. Rather than turning to God in repentance or showing some signs of a change in his ways of thinking, he reverts to his former state of anger. Once again he cries for death.

Again, there is something strangely incongruous about such a request. It is clear that Jonah's wish for death is not related to his discomfort in the face of the elements. God's question to him indicates that his anger is related to the fact that his plant has been destroyed. How strange: He loses only the shade of a small bush and he wishes for death. Something more is obviously at stake here than the loss of a shade tree.

What Jonah perceives in the situation is something strange about the way in which God acts. He is a God who not only has mercy upon those who are thoroughly wicked, but, as soon he he has given a little thought to the comfort of his servant, promptly makes life miserable for him again. If God cannot be fair in at least an elementary way then one is simply at the mercy of a capricious, arbitrary force. Death is to be preferred to life in such a case.

Jonah has now gotten to the point where (unlike in 4:3) he no longer asks God to assist him in the death he desires. He directs this last request only to himself (literally, "he asked his life to expire"). God can apparently no longer even be depended upon to take his life. He would prefer to keep Jonah alive and miserable.

A closer look at God's question in 4:9 also helps us see the gravity of the loss of the shade tree for Jonah. The earlier question that God asked Jonah is now repeated in a slightly different form. In 4:4 it was, in essence: Is it right for you to be angry over the deliverance of the Ninevites? Now, however, the question is related not to God's act of deliverance, but to his act of destruction: Is it right for you to be angry about the destruction of the plant? By his anger Jonah again calls into question the rightness of God's action. He presumes to bring God before the bar of justice and pronounce a verdict of guilty: God's actions are not just.

It is important to see that 4:9 broadens the scope of the issue between God and Jonah in relating the discussion to God's actions cf destruction. The *sphere* of God's activity under discussion is shown here to be limited not merely to Nineveh, but includes Jonah (Israel) as well. Here it is Jonah's *own* experience of destruction at the hands of God that is challenged as to its rightness. What makes Jonah even more angry here and wish even more intensely for death is his perception of the contrasting ways of God's dealings with him (that is, his own people) and Nineveh. God is not just.

The intensity of Jonah's reaction is probably to be related to a comparable experience on the part of those Israelites whom Jonah typifies (see above, Chapter II). They had suffered at the hands of many people, not least the foreign power (probably Persia) to which they were subject. On the other hand, these tormentors were escaping the just reward of their evil deeds (see Malachi 1:2-5, 3:15).

But the author drives home his point in the final verses of the book. The gifts of God were *given* to them in the first place, quite apart from whether or not they deserved them (quite apart from the question of justice). Therefore, if they should lose such gifts or if comparable gifts should be given to others, the question of the fairness of God's action is not an appropriate question. The details of the argument run as follows:

The dilemma set by God for Jonah by his question in 4:9 can be seen more clearly after a consideration of 4:10. Here God indicates to Jonah that the plant has come to him as a pure gift (which, in the final analysis, is true of everything). It was not something which Jonah had coming to him, that he had deserved or earned. It was not something which he had created or even nurtured. Besides, the plant was ephemeral, growing up and perishing in a day. Jonah's ties to the plant were obviously superficial. Moreover, it was only a single plant, and lifeless at that (the ancient Israelites believed that, unlike animals and human beings, plants were lifeless. See Genesis 1). At every point this stands in contrast to God's relationship to Nineveh. He has created and nurtured them, and this over a long period of time. There are large masses of them, both human beings and cattle, and they are full of life.

What is the point made by this recital? It serves to demonstrate that there can be no question of injustice whatsoever in God's taking of the plant from Jonah. We cannot even refer to it as Jonah's plant! Jonah had no claim on the plant whatsoever. He had no *right* to make any claims regarding it. All of his appeals to justice were simply out of court. Judgments regarding caprice on the grounds of what was due Jonah were not in order. Jonah could not lift himself out of the totality of life in which he was inextricably enmeshed to the point of being able to make claims upon that life in its diverse aspects. He was not in any position to make judgments regarding life and death. He is creature, not Creator.

The dilemma posed for Jonah by God's question in 4:9 can now be seen more clearly. Is it right for you to be angry about the plant? If Jonah's answer is negative (as it should have been), then, of course, he thereby admits that he cannot make judgments concerning what God has done with Nineveh. On the other hand, if Jonah's answer is affirmative (as it indeed was), then he tacitly recognizes *God's* right to do what he wills regarding Nineveh! [2]

The final verses drive the point home. Jonah actually was in no position to make final demands or judgments about the plant, therefore he certainly was not in any position to make ultimate demands or judgments about Nineveh. But, once having placed himself in such a position through his regret over the plant, he should certainly recognize God's sovereign right to spare Nineveh.

God has the right to do what pleases him regarding Nineveh because he is Creator. Jonah cannot bring God into court on the question of justice or injustice, mercy or condemnation. He is creature. Thus the argument of the final verses of Jonah move from creation to God's rights as sovereign Lord over his world.

The Wideness of God's Mercy

A further look must now be taken at the last verse of the book. It has been common to translate verse 11, "And *should* not I pity . . ." and to see here a statement regarding God's universal compassion for his creatures. An affirmative answer to the final question is considered obvious by commentators. This, however, implies an "oughtness" or an inevitability to God's pitying action. This would compromise God's sovereign freedom as well as make human responsibility for mission finally unnecessary (God will deliver everybody anyway). It thus seems best to translate, "May not I have pity . . ." (i.e., am I not allowed to have pity?).

The meaning of the word "pity" is not altogether certain. We have seen (Chapter III) that it perhaps has the sense of "moved to spare." As such, this is not an abstract statement about God's continual love for his creatures, but about his being moved to spare Nineveh in this particular instance. In other instances God has *not* been moved to spare (see Jeremiah 13:14; 21:7; Ezekiel 5:11; 7:4, 9). Three questions now need to be asked. What right does God have to be moved to spare Nineveh, given their wickedness? What motivates God to spare Nineveh? What is involved in God's being moved to spare?

We have already dealt with the first question in some detail as we traced the argument of these final verses in the chapter. God is Creator and as such has the sovereign right to respond as he has to Nineveh's repentance, no matter how deserving of judgment they were. But more than that, such action is absolutely consistent with the way in which he has responded to Jonah (Israel).

The second question concerns God's motivation: *Why* does God repent of his decision to destroy Nineveh? It is clear from the message of the book as a whole that God is not moved to spare Nineveh *apart from* their repentance. God "repented of the evil which he had said he would do to them," but *only when* "he saw what they did, how they turned from their evil way" (3:10).

But this is not the only motivating factor for God.[3] It is the presence in the city of the masses of ignorant persons, 120,000 people who have not yet reached the age where they can be considered responsible for the city's violence in any real way. (The sensitivity of the Ninevites' response in Chapter 3 suggests that the reference here is to children rather than to the people as a whole.) Moreover, the city is populated by non-human creatures who would inevitably be caught up in any destruction that befell the human inhabitants. God is moved by the needs of his creatures, both human and non-human (see Exodus 2:23-25; Acts 7:34). He hears their groaning. He sees their plight. This moves him to take pity upon them (see Mark 6:34).

But the fundamental factor which motivates God to act is his steadfast love. According to Nehemiah 13:22, God is asked to pity (spare) "according to the greatness of his steadfast love" (see Jonah 4:2). God in his love desires life for his creatures, not death. For God so loved the Ninevites that . . .[4]

We must be sure not to lose sight of the truth which is present in the reference to the cattle. Non-human creatures, too, are participants in the deliverance which God effects in his world. God's will to save should thus not be so narrowly tied to human beings, as it so often has been. This means, of course, that salvation cannot be understood in any narrow individualistic sense. But, even more, salvation cannot be understood in any sense that could confine it to a community conceived only in terms of human members. God's salvation is cosmic in intention and in scope (see Isaiah 65:17-25; Romans 8:19-23). While human beings may be considered the focus for God's saving work, this final word of the book moves us beyond a narrow concern for our own salvation as human beings to God's broader goals of salvation for his entire world. For God so loved the *world* that . . .

All of this points in the direction of the fact that God's will for his world is salvation and not destruction. He will do all within his power to see that salvation comes rather than destruction. God's love and mercy always have priority over his anger (see Psalm 30:3). He wishes life for his creatures rather than death (see Ezekiel 18:23, 32).

The third and final question now needs to be asked: What is involved in God's being moved to spare? The use of the verb *"moved* to spare" points us to the fact that God's action has its effect upon God himself. This verb has reference to suffering action, action executed with tears in the eyes. See Deuteronomy 19:13, 21; Isaiah 13:18; Ezekiel 5:11; 7:4, 9; where the idea of not having pity is expressed with the figurative language of not allowing tears to flow so as to blunt or deter the judgment. And so "to have pity" would mean action undertaken with "tears flowing down the cheeks." It is suffering action. Here God takes upon *himself* the evil of Nineveh. He bears the weight of its violence, the pain of a thousand plundered cities, including Israel's. God chooses to suffer in place of Nineveh. His tears flow instead of theirs. Someday he may even choose to die.

The book ends with a question. It means to leave the reader with a question. It is the same question that is left with us at the end of Jesus' parable of the vineyard in Matthew 20:15, "Am I not allowed to do what I choose with what belongs to me? Do you begrudge my generosity?" (see Matthew 18:32-33).[5]

And how did Jonah answer the question? Did he remain angry and unrepentant? Did he take his own life? Did he come to recognize the "wideness of God's mercy?" We hear no more about him. The author intends that every Jonah will have to answer the question for himself.

Notes

1. For Chapter 4, see my "Jonah and Theodicy."

2. Leucke, pp. 38-39.

3. Wolff, p. 124.

4. Warshaw, pp. 194, 204: "Mercy is not merely a capricious and negative suspension of law and order, but is an affirmative act of love. . . . love is more important than law and order."

5. Luther, pp. 51-52, 93-94, already interprets Jonah in the light of this parable of Jesus.

X

JONAH

FOR TODAY:

TWO HOMILIES

Mercy and Mission

It's not fair. In fact, I'm tempted to say that it's just plain wrong.

The pastor paid a visit and the 73-year-old neighbor of mine has been converted on his death-bed.

He'd never lived a decent day in his life. Never darkened the church door. Never contributed a penny to charity. Was forever blanketing his neighbors with torrents of spite and disagreeableness. Was forever cursing those "welfare-chiselers" and "drunken Indians" with whom he had to do business. He uttered the name of Jesus Christ more than any Christian, always in anger.

And now in the last hours of his life, all of that has been forgiven. He's home free.

It just doesn't seem right. Certainly the Supreme Court, if it had the chance, would reverse the decision. But God treated him in a way no different from that in which he has treated me, a reasonably faithful and obedient servant my whole life long. Certainly my long-term commitment should make some difference when it comes to the wages at the end of the day. Apparently not. His grace has been extended to that scoundrel in a quality and a quantity the same as that given me.

The conclusion seems inescapable. God is far too indulgent a father. When it comes to turning on the mercy, he doesn't seem to be able to help himself.

It seems unfair, but perhaps the problem lies with us. God has given us the task of mission. Maybe we've failed in the way we have structured that responsibility. God has established a moral order in this world, of which our system of justice is a reasonably good reflection. Should not this system provide important guidelines for establishing our priorities in mission:

• Concentrate that activity among those who have violated the moral order the least. First offenders deserve more mercy than chronic criminals.

• Concentrate on those who have the greatest chance of being rehabilitated. The proffering of mercy cannot be unrelated to effort, time and money.

• Concentrate on those who will be of greatest value to society after rehabilitation. Like the educated, the respectable, and especially those who cherish our traditions in most other respects. Mercy seems to be in order here, obviously. The future, *our* future, is at stake.

• But, most basically, let the punishment fit the crime. This would involve ignoring those who flaunt their wickedness, or at best making halfhearted efforts. That is, let judgment fall and justice be done by channeling your serious efforts elsewhere. Such people deserve the consequences of their evil deeds.

My 73-year-old neighbor? The pastor should have stayed in his study. Or, at the most, pronounced a condemning word of judgment. But only that. And then gone home and watched the fire and brimstone from his picture window.

In the final analysis, then, it may be up to us. We should use care so that we do not provide unwarranted occasions in which God cannot but act in a merciful way. We should circumscribe the field of God's mercy, we should superintend its operation, we should see to it that opportunities do not arise for it to be used in an unfair manner. Trips to Tarshish may be in *God's* own best interests at times. None will then be able to accuse him of being unfair or unjust. And, besides, the world will be saved for democracy.

We never seem to learn. The kingdom of God cannot be compared with IBM and its labor relations board or to a democratic republic with its judicial system. In their own spheres such orders have their proper place. The community and its judges, in letting the punishment fit the crime, are necessary guardians of moral responsibility. They witness to a moral order that must command deep respect. But, even if they carefully take into account the differences among persons in their application of justice, they only begin to approximate what is involved in the mercy of God.

The good news of God's mercy goes beyond justice. Here careful calculations of the relationship between what has been done and what is deserved as a consequence are blatantly put aside. The rules associated with individual responsibility and one's proper dues are broken. God creatively and miraculously intervenes into the system of retributive justice and breaks it wide open. He is gracious toward those who deserve nothing but punishment. He bestows favors quite disproportionate to just desserts. He welcomes the prodigal home without exacting a penalty. He extends salvation on the wicked city (which repents!) in the same way as he has on Jonah, on those who have "borne the burden of the day and the scorching heat" (Matthew 20:12). God looks beyond the sinful actions to the persons, to the masses (4:11), those created in his image, and has mercy. Such love is costly, however, for God takes the burden of guilt on himself.

It is precisely this understanding of mercy, this way beyond the orders of justice, that is needed to set the priorities for Jonah's mission and ours.

All of this implies a recognition that when it comes to *just* desserts, Jonah and all of his counterparts deserve nothing but judgment. They, too, have been made the recipients of God's "lack of fairness." *All* are the recipients of God's unwarranted generosity. A verdict such as, "He has made his bed and now he must lie in it!", must never inform our mission considerations, for God has not insisted on that with us.

This means that the children of God are to be animated by an unswerving purpose to seek and save that which is lost, no matter how perverse, or corrupt or repugnant such persons or societies may be.

This means that we must move beyond a careful calculation which relates priorities to what is empirically evident (e.g., appearance, actions, past experiences) to a high valuation of all persons. All are equally God's creatures whom he loves and whom he desires to incorporate into the community called out by his name.

This means that our priorities must be made in complete independence of special fondnesses we may have for certain other people, special affinities we may have with others, or special approval we may give to certain aspects of the lives of others.

The entire world of God's creation is given to us as a field of vision. Because all are the object of God's love and concern, they are to be the object of our love and concern. No matter who. If Jonah, then everyone! If Nineveh, then the world! Even the cows.

On Thinking About Your Faith

"It really doesn't make any difference what you believe, as long as you are sincere," so some would say. Others might put it this way: "There is a variety of ways of formulating the meaning of the faith which is yours. It really doesn't make too much difference how this is done, or what your resultant beliefs are, just as long as you confess that Jesus Christ is Lord. As Jonah said to the sailors: 'I am a Hebrew and I fear the Lord, the God of heaven, who made the sea and the dry land.'"

A closely related perspective runs like this: "It's dangerous to think too much about your faith. If you engage the rational process too much, you risk losing the faith you have. You should be satisfied with the simple beliefs instilled in you since childhood. Hold on to them firmly, and watch out for those who ask questions about what you hold dear." Like God: "Is it right for you to be angry?"

Or, those in positions of pastoral leadership might say it like this: "When it comes to talking with people about their faith, don't rock the boat. If you get to asking too many questions about the meaning of the Christian faith, you may get the people all confused and destroy their childlike faith. By and large be content with positive reinforcement. Preach and teach in such a way that your people will become more and more pleased and satisfied with the way in which they have always been thinking about the faith which is theirs." Jonah must have had such a pastor.

Or, perhaps the matter takes a somewhat more sophisticated tone: "When it comes to living your Christian life, it is much more important to do than to think. Thinking is ivory-tower stuff. When it comes to being a faithful witness to Jesus Christ, you don't want to go off on some head trip. The important work for God is out there in the real world, feeding the hungry, comforting the bereaved, counseling the distraught, teaching the children. And it is, of course, only in the doing that you learn how to think properly about the faith anyway." Like taking ships to Tarshish.

Or, perhaps one's perspective might take this twist: "In the Christian life what is important is not so much how you think as how you feel. It's the heart that counts, not the head. Thinking about the faith too much is dangerous because it has a tendency to moderate all those feelings of wonderfulness. The really important matter is whether your life has a certain glow, radiates a certain joy, reflects a certain peace, all defined in terms of a surpassing and perpetual feeling of well-being." Like preferring to live rather than die.

But one of the things Jonah has to teach us is that the way we think about the faith, no matter how little (and we cannot avoid that), and the beliefs we hold, no matter how simple, will have much to say both about the way we act and the way we feel in the living out of the Christian life. That is to say, your theology will often determine whether in certain situations you obey God or disobey him, whether you are joyful or despondent. This has been well illustrated in modern surveys which show that there are clear correlations between one's theology and one's daily actions and attitudes (see *A Study of Generations*).

Jonah was a man of faith. He was a member of the covenant community. In fact, he was a prophetic leader of that community. As such he was commissioned by God to carry out a task of mission. He refused. He refused, however, not because he had no or little faith in God, but because his simplistic *thinking* about his faith was wrongheaded. He fled not because of unbelief, but because of a simple, but unexamined, belief with which he (and most of his contemporaries) had been nurtured since childhood.

It ran something like this. The guilty should be punished according to their just desserts. They should not be allowed to escape judgment. For God to allow for other possibilities, to be merciful toward people who deserved judgment, would wreak moral havoc on the world.

It was just such a belief, such a simplistic way of thinking about God's ways with his world, that led Jonah, first of all, into disobedience and then, finally, into despair.

"I cannot obey the call to go to Nineveh. They deserve only judgment. To preach to them makes for the possibility of repentance and God, being the merciful God that he is, might commute the deserved sentence. That must not be. My understanding of the faith in this instance calls for 'religious disobedience.' "

Jonah has thus articulated the meaning of his faith in such a way that it becomes impossible for him to respond in obedience in this situation. Jonah is thus disobedient because his theology has gone bad at one point. The problem for Jonah thus becomes, not so much his disobedience of the call, but his theology. The former was only a symptom. And so, even when Jonah is obedient and does go to Nineveh, the problem is revealed as unresolved: Jonah is angry rather than joyful at the Ninevites' repentance and deliverance.

This, in turn, leads to a second result of Jonah's incorrect thinking about his faith. He becomes quite despondent because of what happens and asks God to kill him. Jonah's theology has led him into utter despair. If he had had his theological head on straight, he would rather have rejoiced with the angels in heaven and cherished life.

The marvelous thing to watch in the book is how God goes to the root of his problem, his theology. Good pastoral counselor that he is, God does not treat him for disobedience or despair; he treats him for a case of bad theology.

God's treatment for such, in the final analysis, is theological discussion (see Chapter I). The shape which God's mercy takes with Jonah in this situation is a theological conversation. If and when the theological issue is resolved, the disobedience and the despair will take care of themselves.

All of this should lead us to think seriously about our lives as children of God:

a) We regularly need to examine and re-examine the way in which we understand our faith, the beliefs we hold dear, and the effect they may have on our actions and feelings.

b) We must learn to recognize that the task of mission, of evangelism, of "soul-care," may entail, first and foremost, theological conversation.

c) We need to learn that the task of thinking about our faith is an important means by which God works out his gracious purposes in our lives.

BIBLIOGRAPHY

Allen, L. C. *The Books of Joel, Obadiah, and Jonah and Micah,* Eerd-mans, 1976.

Brockington, L. H. "Jonah," *Peake's Commentary on the Bible,* Nelson, 1962, pp. 627-29.

Burrows, M. "The Literary Category of the Book of Jonah." *Translating and Understanding the Old Testament,* ed. by H. Frank and W. Reed. Abingdon, 1971, pp. 80-107.

Clements, R. "The Purpose of the Book of Jonah." *Supplements to Vetus Testamentum* 28 (1975), pp. 16-28.

Glaze, A. J. Jr., "Jonah." *The Broadman Bible Commentary,* Broadman Press, 1972, pp. 152-82.

Good, E. M. *Irony in the Old Testament,* SPCK, 1965, pp. 1-55.

Knight, G. *Ruth and Jonah.* Rev. ed., SCM Press, 1966.

Landes, G. "The Kerygma of the Book of Jonah." *Interpretation* 28 (1967), pp. 3-31.

Luecke, R. *Violent Sleep.* Fortress, 1969, pp. 3-45.

Luther, Martin. *Lectures on the Minor Prophets (II): Jonah and Habakkuk.* Vol. 19, Luther's Works, Concordia, 1974.

McGowan, Jean. "Jonah." *The Jerome Bible Commentary,* Prentice-Hall, 1968, pp. 633-37.

Miskotte, K. H. *When the Gods Are Silent,* tr. by J. Doberstein, Harper, 1967, pp. 422-38.

Murphy, R. E. "The Book of Jonah." *The Interpreter's One-Volume Commentary.* Abingdon, 1971, pp. 480-82.

Myers, J. M. "The Book of Jonah." *The Layman's Bible Commentary,* vol. 14, John Knox Press, 1959, pp. 160-76.

Robinson, D. W. B. "Jonah." *The New Bible Commentary Revised,* Eerdmans, 1970, pp. 746-51.

Smart, James. "The Book of Jonah." *The Interpreter's Bible,* vol. 6, Abingdon, 1956, pp. 871-94.

Warshaw, T. S. "The Book of Jonah," *Literary Interpretations of Biblical Narratives,* ed. by K. Gros Louis, Abingdon, 1974, pp. 191-207.

Watts, J. D. W. *The Books of Joel, Obadiah, Jonah, Nahum, Habakkuk and Zephaniah,* Cambridge, 1975, pp. 72-97.

Wolff, H. W. *Studien zum Jonabuch.* Neukirchen, 1965. The last three chapters of this book appear in English translation in *Currents in Theology and Mission,* 1976, pp. 4-19, 86-97, 141-50.)

Wolff, H. W. Commentary on Jonah, forthcoming in Biblischer Kommentar and Hermeneia series.